MONSOON MOSQUES

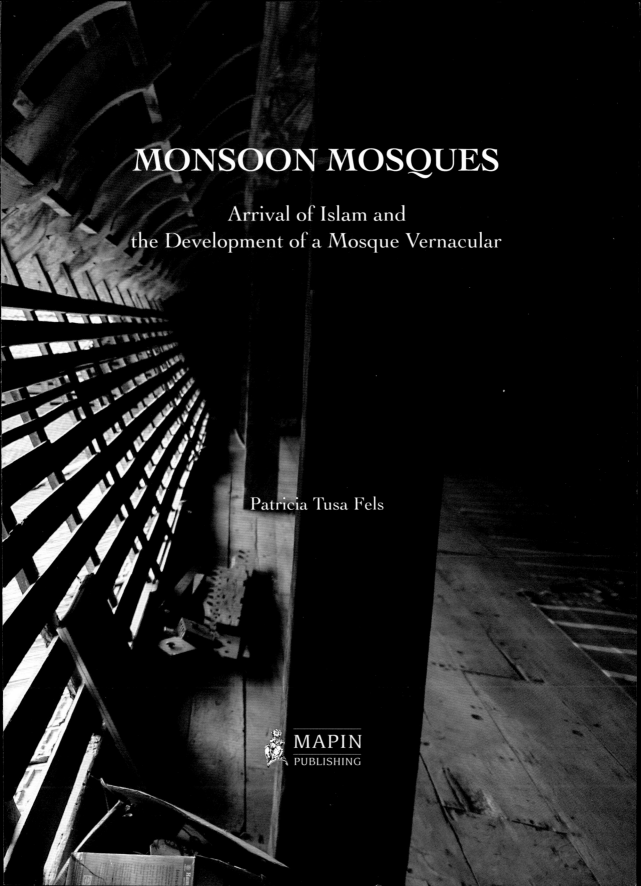

MONSOON MOSQUES

Arrival of Islam and
the Development of a Mosque Vernacular

Patricia Tusa Fels

MAPIN
PUBLISHING

First published in India in 2020 by

Mapin Publishing

International Distribution
North America
ACC Art Books
T: +1 800 252 5231 • F: +1 212 989 3205
E: ussales@accartbooks.com • www.accartbooks.com/us/

United Kingdom, Europe and Asia
John Rule Art Book Distribution
40 Voltaire Road,
London SW4 6DH
T: +44 020 7498 0115
E: johnrule@johnrule.co.uk • www.johnrule.co.uk

Rest of the World
Mapin Publishing Pvt. Ltd
706 Kaivanna, Panchvati, Ellisbridge
Ahmedabad 380006 INDIA
T: +91 79 40 228 228 • F: +91 79 40 228 201
E: mapin@mapinpub.com • www.mapinpub.com

Text © Patricia Tusa Fels
Photographs © Don & Patricia Fels, except those
listed below:
Feroze Babu: pp. 22, 23 (top), 43, 45, 51
Krishnan Nair Studios: p. 109
Manish Chalana: p. 34
Benjamin Fels: p. 44
Plans and drawings: Patricia Fels, Shweta Bhatia Gupta,
and Mapin Design Studio

ISBN: 978-93-85360-70-1

Copyediting: Neha Manke / Mapin Editorial
Design: Darshit Mori and Gopal Limbad /
   Mapin Design Studio
Production: Mapin Design Studio
Printed in China

NOTE ON TRANSLITERATION

It is difficult to be consistent when dealing with sources from English, Malayalam, Hindi, Indonesian, Javanese, Malay and Arabic. Over the centuries there have been different spellings and varied interpretations. Mosque name-boards will have one spelling outside the building and another inside. Mosques are referred to as masjid, *palli, mesjid*. I have tried to use the terms most current and hopefully most commonly used by the local people.

PAGES 2–3 Wooden louvers at Jami Masjid, Kozhikode, Kerala

PAGES 6–7 Detail of wood beam connections at the veranda of Masjid Agung Surakarta, Java

For the many men and women who
opened the doors of their mosques and
generously shared their memories.

Contents

INTRODUCTION

Islam and the Sea
Trade Routes and the Spread of a New Religion

⌒

"What we initially call history is nothing more than a narrative."

Michel de Certeau, *The Writing of History*, 287

*"…by seeking to move forward, we find ourselves looking back and discovering
with some surprise from when we've come."*

Ralph Ellison, *Collected Essays*, 593

*"…before the arrival of the Portuguese in the Indian Ocean in 1498 there
had been no organized attempt by any political power to control
the sea-lanes and the long-distance trade of Asia…
the Chinese empire and the successive dynasties of the Indian subcontinent were fully occupied
in upholding their political and economic power over unbroken* terra firma *and never
seriously considered overseas colonial ventures as logical corollaries of seaborne trade."*

Chaudhuri 1985, 14–15

For millennia, the exotic spices that grow in tropical Asia have been objects of desire around the globe. These spices were freely traded between the peoples of Arabia, China, India and Southeast Asia, until the Europeans arrived seeking control over the trade. Spices grown in India and Southeast Asia were shipped across the sea to the Arabian Peninsula. Once unloaded from ships, the prized cargo was transported by camel overland, then brought by sail across the Mediterranean to Italy. From Italy the aromatic spices spread to all of Europe. Typically, along the maritime spice route contacts between the adherents of different religions were peaceful. When Arab merchants of the Yemenite coast became Muslim, they (and the learned men who followed) passed on their faith to the peoples living along the Arabian Sea. In the seventh century, merchants of Arabia had already been trading with the people of southwestern India for hundreds of years. The movement of Islam to Sumatra, the Malay Peninsula, Java and other

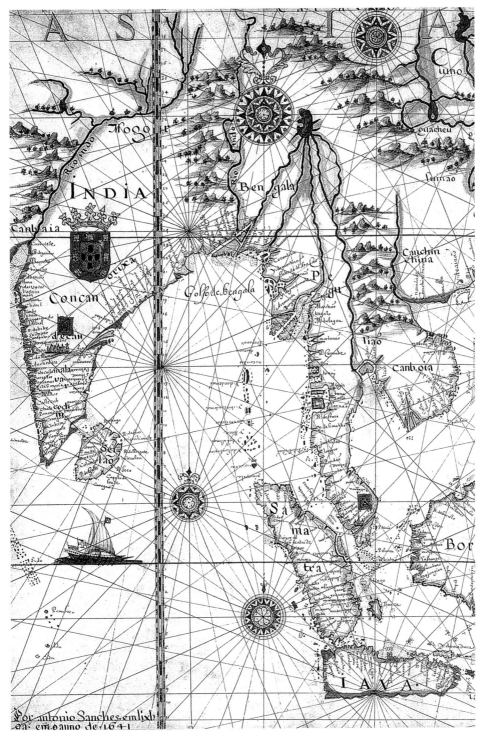

Portolan map, Antonio Sanches, 1641. *Idrographisiae Nova Descriptio* (Koninklijke Bibliotheck, The Hague)

ports of Southeast Asia charted a similar pattern. "The places where Islam established early and deep roots were those closest to international trade routes…" (Kaplan 2010, 244) Following centuries-old trading routes, Islam moved with the trade winds to the spice trading ports.

As seafaring societies developed, their religious practices changed. Waves of religion followed the trade. Animist practices throughout Southeast Asia were altered by Hindu and Buddhist influences from India. A series of Hindu-Buddhist empires ruled portions of the Indonesian archipelago for the centuries preceding the arrival of Islam. The Srivijaya Empire, based in Sumatra, controlled much of Malaysia and Java until the 12th century. Starting in the late 13th century, the Javanese Majapahits extended their reign to the far edges of the archipelago.

Along the Malabar Coast (present-day Kerala), Islam was integrated into a society where Hinduism remained strong. In parts of Sumatra and Malaysia, entire villages, cities and communities converted and Hindu-Buddhist worship, for the most part, disappeared. In Java, an analogous process occurred along the coast and then inland, followed by the foundation of Islamic kingdoms, culminating in the Mataram Sultanate of the 16th century.

The spread of Islam was slow and steady, the wind blowing the religion and the spices (along with cloth and exotic forest products) from port to port. The spice trade became far more than a trade in commodities. A grand transfer of religious culture, people and native plants took place. Moluccan nutmeg and cloves, Kerala pepper ("black gold") and cardamom, Ceylon cinnamon, Arabian coffee, Chinese tea, and Southeast Asian ginger were transported from their original settings and grown throughout tropical Asia. Religious conversion was usually voluntary and Islam spread from Muslim men marrying local women, merchants introducing others to their new faith, and conversions of local people by visiting Sufi wise men. Along the sea routes the overland invading armies of Central Asia that swept through north India were replaced by peaceful (and non-conquering) maritime traders and travelling religious teachers.

In tropical Asia, Islam became a religion that was adopted and adapted to fit the place.

Richard Eaton describes it:

> "From the seventh century on, Muslims everywhere had been engaged in projects of cultural accommodation, appropriation, and assimilation, which had the effect of transforming what had begun as an Arab cult into what we call a world religion. … the whole of Islamic history can be seen as a venture consisting of the many ways that people living in different ages and cultures managed, without rejecting their local cultures, to incorporate into their lives a normative order as they understood it to have been revealed in the Qur'an." (2003, 4)

In the 2009 series of essays, *Islamic Connections*, scholars and academics from across the world debated and discussed the "Islamization of Southeast Asia". The authors stated: "as yet, there has been no serious work done that discusses the historical dynamics of Islamization in South and Southeast Asia as part of interconnected processes of social transformation." (Feener 2009, xvi). The authors wanted to dismiss the dominant theories of influence that go in only one direction, west to east. In the history of the Indian Ocean littoral, connections to the sea dominated. A two-way transfer of goods and ideas was the norm. While Islam, of course, came from the Arabian Peninsula, much was altered and / or carried back. The religion was transformed in each location into a regional Muslim faith. There have been many attempts to set out one grand theory of the development of Islam throughout the Indian Ocean basin. One inclusive idea cannot 'explain' the history. Just as kingdoms rose and fell, port locations moved over time, religions appeared and disappeared; the entire process was messy, complex and varied.

Sebastian Prange's contribution to the *Islamic Connections* conference specifically pinpoints the numerous connections between Malabar and Southeast Asian spice ports. The various spices that brought such great wealth were the native plants of these regions. Besides being the origins of the spices, the Malabar Coast and the Straits of Malacca are geographic nodes between the different monsoon winds. Because of dependence on seasonal winds, the ports became forced resting points in the movement between continents. These intersection points were the entry ports for Islam into South India and Southeast Asia.

If the history of Islamization along the Indian Ocean trade routes is to remain open to new research, so too should the study of the physical signs of residency. Early scholars viewed the culture of Southeast Asia as derivative of India or China, now most have realized "that much of Southeast Asian art and architecture revealed quintessentially indigenous conceptions of sanctity." (Daud Ali, *Islamic Connections*, 5) While "the mosque was still needed to proclaim the Islamic identity of a town…the architectural idiom could not always be kept in orthodox mode. By the time Islam reaches the Indonesian archipelago and the fringes of China, the architectural details of the mosques underwent a near-complete transformation…" (Chaudhuri 1990, 346)

In Malabar and then coastal Southeast Asia, religious structures became splendid creations of rising wooden roofs, an elaboration on the local timber construction techniques. This book presents a group of buildings little studied and not typically considered together.[1] The mosques visually represent an 'appropriation' of a local vernacular, buildings based on local needs and available materials. The religion came from the sea, the mosques arose out of the earth of each unique place.

The geography produced certain consistent similarities. Cultural traditions produced unique differences. Kerala mosques adopted the styles of the big wooden temples, palaces and homes of the Malabar Coast. The Malaysian and Indonesian mosques followed a similar trajectory—adapting parts of the local vernacular and creating a house for prayer that was comfortable in the extreme climate and made of local materials. All appropriated the big rain-shedding roof of the tropics, pyramids of wood that rise to reach the skies. In a perceptive lecture, the Indonesian architecture professor Josef Prijotomo told of studying old manuscripts where "architecture is

---

1. One of the few exceptions is Mehrdad Shokoohy who thoroughly examins the mosques of South India and devotes a chapter in *Muslim Architecture of South India* to their connections with the mosques of Southeast Asia.

formulated as entering the shade under a tree, and not as a shelter." Similarly, in India, architect Charles Correa has written an essay, "A Place in the Sun", which is really about the need for a place in the shade (the actual title of a book of his essays). Correa speaks of the importance of knowing where you are and respecting your local climate and culture. Both men see the roof as a central component of a tropical architecture.

Before the arrival of Islam, a very particular way of building had developed in the coastal tropics of Asia, an area of penetrating heat and intense rains. Long shorelines backed by mountains and hills received ample rain from semi-annual monsoons. Great forests grew and spice plants thrived. The

forests had abundant wood for building boats and houses. Some of these timber species were resistant to bugs and thus were especially valued for construction. People of the tropics needed a place where they were protected from the sun and the rain. Over time they invented ways to increase the coolness inside. Venting roofs, open floors, porous walls—all provided a system of air movement that made sitting in the roofed space a pleasing experience. These grand structures with tiered roofs and open colonnades served the needs of royalty, religion and residents.

The tropical mosques of the spice trade routes are a direct reflection of the place (wetlands and hills along a tropical coast with two annual

The five-tiered roof at Masjid Limo Kaum, Sumatra

monsoons), the materials available (abundant wood and local stone), and the religious custom (the need for a sizeable hall for prayer, which protects the people from the heat of the sun and the intensity of the rain). They stand as powerful and visible expressions of the integration of Islam into the culture of tropical Asia. Large wood-framed roofs and fine wooden craftsmanship distinguish this vernacular, a typology I call the "monsoon mosque". This is not a rigid typology but a collection of living, responsive forms; what Christopher Alexander describes as "…good architecture…well adapted to context, the product of many decisions about form which were tried and tested as those who lived and used buildings sought to adapt them to their purpose."

Looking at these mosques we see the wealth of spice traders, the elegance of royalty and the humbleness of the rice-farming villagers. Since Islam has no central authority like the Catholic Vatican, mosque building was always funded locally. In Kerala and in the trading ports of Java patrons were typically wealthy merchants, in Sumatra villagers built communally. Throughout the littoral, immigrants banded together with local converts to create prayer halls. In central Java, royalty funded a remarkable series of mosques. The scale varies but the ability to craft wood into a place of beauty, an oasis for prayer, remains consistent throughout the spice trading coasts. In the panorama of the Asian trading networks, the tropical mosque is a unique by-product, a

Mithqal Palli, Kozhikode, Kerala

physical reminder of what was once a complex set of international mercantile connections that thrived without telegraph, telephone or Internet. Islam served as a unifying force for large-scale commercial trade and created a chain of caravan and maritime routes that joined far-off ports on the Indian Ocean to the Mediterranean.

Travel anywhere in the southern lands of Asia today and it will be quickly evident that physical evidence of this illustrious chapter of history has almost completely vanished. Many of the fine old mosque buildings have been demolished and replaced by generic concrete structures. It is a quirk of history and economics that some have survived in Kerala and Indonesia; in most of tropical Asia, the mosques of centuries past have completely disappeared. The survivors could be put on the endangered species list, if such a categorization existed.

Scholars will continue to debate the exact dates of the arrival of Islam, but the stories of the first mosques don't need precise times. Throughout the centuries the mosques have been built and rebuilt. Over time the mosque communities did add some Western elements, but mainly they sustained the inherent structure of the original mosques. These early mosques are an excellent example of a building typology created from the existing systems of a place. The carriers of the new religion were most interested in a place to pray and embraced local traditions, feeling little need to impose the architecture of another locale.

Following the paths of Ibn Battuta, Cheng Ho and many other adventurers of the early centuries, we will travel from spice port to spice port, sometimes venturing into the interior. This trade can be

followed even further back to Greco-Roman times through the 1st century AD *Periplus Maris Erythraei*, a manual of trade and navigation. We know from these writings that ships from the Middle East were able to sail directly across the Indian Ocean to ports such as Muziris in Malabar and from there to the "Land of Gold" (Sumatra).

Rarely mentioned in architectural surveys, the mosques' lack of recognition exposes a persistent prejudice against the humble vernacular. The surviving mosques often serve poor communities in historic city centres. Far from the world of international historic preservation the congregations struggle with maintaining their mosques. Only in parts of Indonesia are the old mosques (*masjid tua*) celebrated as a national treasure. But even there, and throughout Malabar and Malaysia, these fine old buildings are being remodelled with faraway design elements. The replacement mosques display little of the local traditions, with only the slightest of a nod to regional history, climate, or customs.

Today, the majority of adults living in urban cities cannot imagine designing and building their own home, office, church or school. In order to understand vernacular architecture, one must step away from the world of processed food, structures and transport. When the mosques discussed here were built, people built their own houses, and together they built their places of worship. Many grew their own food and gathered the materials with which they built the structures of their village or town. In the story of Islamic conversion, a point was reached where the people needed to build a structure for a new use, a hall for prayer. In the beginning converts met and prayed outside. But when a donor or a community came forth with funding, there was a need to decide what form the new building should take. In this pre-literate society, the tendency would be to look around and use what material is available with what the craftsmen knew. In Kerala, Indonesia and Malaysia, there were forms that could be adapted for building a mosque: borrowed from houses, community meeting places, temples and pavilions. For many years the Europeans tried to find an outside source for the mosque. Their assumption was that the mosque must have come from somewhere else. Were the colonialists so distracted that they could not see the talents and resources of the local people?

It might be obligatory but it is certainly not sufficient to list the number of columns and their size or to describe the facade. There is so much more residing in the old mosques. Edmund de Waal in *The Hare with Amber Eyes* describes it well: "You have to develop a way of seeing how a building sits in its landscape or streetscape. You have to discover how much room it takes up in the world, how much of the world it displaces." (22)

I will try and tell a bit of what happened at a particular place, including the history, the symbolism and who worshipped at a mosque. Just as mosques do not face the street but face the distant Makkah, to unearth their stories one must disconnect a bit from day-to-day business. The entrance to a mosque compound is on the street but the prayer hall entry can be opposite or on one side. A non-parallel wall often marks the relationship to the street and the fabric of a village or city. The stories are also askance or doubtful. They have created disagreement amongst scholars or elicited disavowal from locals. Elders have crafted stories diverse from the history books.

Fiction is added to fact, an honoured scholar added to the list of founders. Djinns (ghosts) are rumoured to be in the attic. The goal here is not to dispute stories, or to establish one shining truth. That certain stories have survived for centuries speaks to a probable basis in some facts. This is not a definitive history and it is hoped that the telling of tales will continue. In places where names and spellings are in constant flux, physical structures adjusted constantly, and streets renamed yearly, it would be counterproductive and actually impossible to try and create an irrefutable "truth". The variety and richness of the recountings speak to the vitality of the communities and the mosques they support. The one unquestionable fact is that the Muslim population has played a significant role in Indian Ocean history over many centuries.

This book does not attempt to document all the surviving monsoon mosques. Over thirty mosques were chosen for the book. They all maintain faithfulness to the original condition and they all illustrate the story of the creation of a monsoon mosque vernacular. We will see the importance of ancestral cultures and view a history of tolerance different from much that we hear about today.

We will be able to study the variations, the similarities, and the unique outcroppings. Many more mosques could have been included, but a story will be told and connections will be made. Hopefully, there will be renewed interest in this very special vernacular form.

Mosque Essentials
Space and Spices, Peace and Prayer

———————⌒———————

"I see the vernacular as a dynamic process in which the most refined styles from the past are continually merged with the play-it-by-eye-and-by-ear improvisations which we invent in our efforts to control our environment and entertain ourselves. This is not only in language and literature, but in architecture and cuisine, in music....In it the styles and techniques of the past are adjusted to the needs of the present, and in its integrative action the high styles of the past are democratized. From this perspective the vernacular is, no less than the styles associated with aristocracy, a gesture toward perfection."

Ralph Ellison, *Collected Essays*, 608

"…theory of initial occupancy or first effective settlement, the notion that the first post-pioneer forms established in a landscape are a powerful shaping factor for later generations of builders."

Louis P. Nelson in *Buildings & Landscapes* 20, no.1, 2013

Despite the predominance of the Islam of Arabia in the minds of the general public, the majority of Muslims live in the hot wetlands of tropical Asia. The largest population of Muslims resides in Indonesia, followed by Pakistan and India. Along the tropical lands bordering the Indian Ocean, residents built their structures to provide protection from the heat of the sun and the force of the rains. Long before the arrival of Islam, there existed a way of constructing expansive embracing roofs. The highest roof in village or city marked the most important function, either religious or royal.

This book looks at a unique phenomenon touching spice ports in a specific climate zone. Pepper and cardamom originated in Malabar, cloves and nutmeg in Indonesia, ginger in Southeast Asia. Abundance of rain, richly forested hills, intense heat and humidity—all affected what vegetation grew and how building forms evolved. Mosques built in China, northern India, the Indian east coast or even the East African coast responded to a different vernacular, climate and resources. Although impacted by trade the mosques of those areas evolved using diverse materials and forms. In this book we are examining not only a vernacular

Masjid and tomb complex of Sunan Bayat, Java

but also a process: trade and a new religion joined with a specific climate and building tradition.

Janet Abu-Lughod, in writing about the continuance of traditional architecture, stresses that there is no purely traditional architecture. "Throughout history architectural forms have migrated" from people moving, traders carrying good. She writes that there was "no intrinsic indigenous traditional Islamic architecture that dates back to the time of the Prophet…" (Abu-Lughod 1995, 8) Muslims along the tropical trade routes appear to have been familiar with the local

vernacular and comfortable with adapting it for new houses for prayer. Along with a place to wash, there were two essential elements for the mosque: a delineated hall for prayer and the *mihrab* (a marker for the direction of pray).

From these simple elements developed the grand structures of Persia, Arabia, China and North India and the striking mosques of the monsoon trade route. *Mimbar*s (a raised area for delivering sermons), minarets, porticoes and verandas, courtyards, ablution pools, clocks and lights—all evolved as the religion grew. The first mosque was a residence, meeting centre, place of congregational prayer, education centre, shelter for homeless, legal court, and locus of celebration. It was truly the 'heart' of the community. Many of these functions are now housed separately but, especially in the pavilion mosques of Java, the old mosque compounds still serve as community centres.

Islam in monsoon Asia is directly connected to the Hadhrami Arabs who sailed the seas for centuries and who after their conversion to Islam carried their new religion to faraway ports of call. Unlike the rest of the Arabian Peninsula, the Hadhramaut is affected by the monsoon winds and truly belongs to the world of the Indian Ocean littoral. Interestingly, the majority of Muslim people along the Indian Ocean trade routes follow Sunni Islam and the Shafi'i school of law.[1] In all of northern and central India (and China), most Muslims follow the Hanafi school. In fact, one can colour the map with all the Shafi'i adherents hugging the coast of Yemen, Malabar, East Africa, Sumatra, Malaysia, Java and the rest of Indonesia.

Communal worship, the essence of a mosque's function, meant that the roof grew larger as the size of congregations grew. The daily five prayers required of Muslims can happen anywhere; the mosque serves as a place for prayer, a retreat, and of course, the site of the Friday prayer. The tropical climate mandated a roof. The original mosque, Prophet Muhammad's home in Medina, was a house with a large courtyard and an open portico. In the tropics, because of the monsoon rains, it was necessary to elevate the floor and provide a roof. The Prophet's open courtyard became a raised unadorned interior room. The spirit of a

mosque remains a positive emptiness, a space that fills and unfills, a place that marks time with the five daily calls to prayers.

Throughout Asia orientation of a building involves ancient traditions, with different directions reflecting level of importance, safety, and cosmological concerns. In a mosque the *mihrab*, typically an arched niche, is centred in the *qibla* wall (the wall that faces Makkah). As we will see in the stories of Islam in Java, local people sometimes wanted to adjust this orientation. Only over time were all the new mosques laid out to face the proper degree of west. In the old city centres of Kerala, the palace towns of Java, and the villages of Sumatra, the mosques can often be identified by the visible jogs on street fronts, the angle of one building offset from the main street. Thus, the religious meaning of the building is subtly revealed.

The vernacular tropical mosques that we see today were built (and re-built) between the 14th and early 20th centuries. An enormous amount of wealth was based on the spice trade. Spices built Venetian palaces and Dutch estates, and led to an unheard-of expansion of colonialism. In the days before the arrival of the Europeans, the spice trade was not controlled or dominated by one power. Like the wind, the trade blew in and out, creating giant waves of wealth and troughs of bankruptcy. It was in this period and up until the 19th century that the great timber mosques of the tropical spice trade were built. We can trace the effect of local wealth on the construction of the timber mosques. As trade control moved into the hands of the Europeans, the mosques lost some of their expansive magnificence and became more modest.

---

1. Shafi'i comes from 8th-century Abu Abdullah surnamed Shafi'i who wrote on civil and canonical law and was a Sunni.

The free-standing mosques were constructed by resident masons and carpenters, men well versed in local design idioms and methods. The mosque builders, familiar with the structure of the traditional houses and temples, adapted these styles to create a comfortable house for prayer made of native materials. The craftsmen observed what existed and altered as required to produce an elegant solution for the vast interior space of the mosque prayer hall. It seemed perfectly fitting that the house of prayer would respond to local customs and replicate indigenous building practices.

Wood and stone carving, much-developed artisan skills, were transformed from figurative displays to carvings of plant life and Arabic sacred scripts. Influences from afar are seen in the details— flooring stone imported from the home country, or interior particulars such as the shape of a window or door, or arches at doors and the *mihrab* (coming from Arabia and North India). As transformations in building technology occurred, some new materials or methods were incorporated into traditional techniques. Circulation of men, goods and ideas continued, especially in the old port cities, even though climatic needs remained constant and cultural constraints changed very slowly.

In the tropics (especially in Kerala), the prayer hall is adjacent to some sort of antechamber or entry area. This large front porch formed the entrance to the prayer hall and was also used for prayer. One-storey verandas (or colonnades) were layered onto the composition. These provided shaded space for discussion and/or prayer. As more space was needed, the verandas were often enclosed (Kerala) or expanded (Java). The verandas (or Javanese pavilions) are an enduring element of the monsoon zone. Only in the village mosques of Sumatra do we not find the expansive front porch. The need for expanded mosque space did not occur in the village and thus the original square prayer hall can still be seen, much as it was in the Javanese mosques before the veranda additions.

Prayer hall at Masjid Sunan Bayat, Java

Wooden *mimbar* at Masjid Bingkudu, Sumatra

Except for the early Sumatran and Malaysian mosques, the walls of the mosque were built of the porous, easily worked and abundant local stone (Kerala) or brick (Java) and plastered in mud and lime plaster. This combination had proven itself over generations. The walls literally breathed. A granite plinth raised the structure above the ground for protection from dampness, monsoon floods and insects. In Sumatra, the structure was elevated on wood posts, and constructed with a wood floor, walls and interior columns. In Java and Kerala, the interior columns were timber with a stone plinth. Every once in a while, a mosque displays granite columns, which were a popular variant for temples. Wooden brackets cap the columns, the more elaborate the carvings the more prestigious the building. As availability of timber changed, the shape of the mosque columns was transformed from large sculpted timbers to a simpler slimmer form. In Kerala the interior posts disappeared in later mosques, with floor loads handled by beams spanning from wall to wall. The Keralites framed upper floors with large, exposed,

Carved granite plinth in Java. The prayer rugs have been adjusted to face Makkah as the column (and thus the mosque) is not the proper orientation.

squared off timbers. Joists running perpendicular to the beams combined with floorboards to create a patterned main floor ceiling. Some ceilings have a carved overlay in the form of a coffered ceiling. The island nations took a different route, preferring single-storey mosques constructed with visible layers of roofs rising upwards. The interiors of Indonesian mosques were dramatically vertical. Over time, many mosques have closed off the upper tiers with an interior ceiling. Fortunately, the complexities of a multilayered timber roof can still be seen in some mosques.

LEFT The large veranda pavilion at the Masjid Agung Yogyakarta

RIGHT A single carved wooden column from which eight radiating arms extend out to support the roof structure, Sumatra

Coffered ceiling at Muchundi Palli, Kozhikode

New corrugated metal roofing on the existing wooden framework of the roof at Surau Sheikh Burhanuddin, Sumatra

At the time of the construction of these mosques, dense, insect-resistant wood was abundant in the lush and luxuriant forests of the tropics. High quality timbers came out of the hills. Teak and beautiful jungle woods such as rosewood were transformed into eaves, air vents, columns, rafters, beams and ceilings (India). In Malaysia, *cengal* was the hardwood of choice. The Sumatrans preferred *kayu* or *meranti*, both tropical hardwoods. In surveying the old mosques, a variety of wood species were found. Along with *cengal, kayu* and *meranti*, elders spoke of *seng* wood, *tara juah* (new wood), teak, even coconut and jackfruit.

Besides having a natural resistance to insects these timbers were easily carved. A long tradition of woodworking craftsmanship had developed to serve local industries of boat and building construction. Several mosques contain inscriptions crediting a shipmaster's work. Artisan wood carvers throughout the monsoon zone performed their magic, replicating patterns and standards of indentations and proportion while replacing any reference to human forms with vegetative imagery or calligraphy. Most of the *mimbar*s are of wood, finely carved in a style unique to the monsoon zone. Calligraphy is the most pervasive element in Islamic art. Words gain nobility because of their connection to the Qur'an. The script is transformed into a work of art. The elegant transformation of words in Arabic, Persian, Turkish, Urdu, Malayalam, Javanese, and Malay onto stone or wood demonstrates the long-held belief in the beauty of the written word.

In the local vernacular wood beams and rafters displayed exact joinery. Carpenters used a variety of techniques; mortise and tenon with no nails were often used, along with wood pegs. The roof developed from a simple double pitch to the gabled hip roof and the tiered pyramid roof. Scholars are always conjecturing on what influenced a particular architectural style. Sources for the large, pitched roof are much debated: some suggest southern China, others the wood structures of Nepal, but the probable truth is that the roof form developed independently as a solution to regional conditions. The entire ensemble acted like a huge lung, allowing air in and out of the building while keeping water out. In addition, man has always looked up for inspiration. Where timber is abundant, it has been transformed into diverse versions of expansive wooden roofs. Throughout the world, in places with no known connections, one finds this exuberant display of roofs on religious buildings. Tiers of roofs mark religious centres, which also function as beacons for the community. They are found not only along the tropical Indian Ocean littoral but in parts of North India, Pakistan, China, Burma, Thailand, and even the far north of Russia and Scandinavia. The roof has served as a bridge between man and the heavens. V.S. Naipaul wrote about a tropical mosque: "Much of the architectural energy of the building had gone into this roof." (70) Construction of the signature

Calligraphy and carvings on beams at Ponnani Jami Masjid, Kerala

timber roof was typical of mosques throughout the tropical areas of Asia. In the monsoon zone the motif of roof as umbrella is ubiquitous; in Kerala and in Java the umbrella has further associations with royalty and power. The grander the scale of the lofty, tiered "crown" of the building, the higher the status was implied.

The wooden superstructure of the mosque has the most layers of complexity; beams, purlins and rafters ascend to the peak. The long-standing idioms of proportion (relation of width to depth to length) and framework were faithfully followed to ensure structural stability. Throughout Indonesia the roof structure was supported by wooden columns. Masonry exterior walls served more as protecting screens than structural units. In Kerala, the stone walls formed part of the structure of

Mortise and tenon beam connections with carved capitals at Masjid Panjunan, Java

TOP Radiating wood rafters at a Kerala mosque

Top tiers of the many tiered Indonesian mosque roof (at Java on the left, Sumatra on right). Many of the carved panels between tiers have been covered but they originally provided an excellent ventilation system.

the space. Indonesians, being well aware of the many earthquakes that shake the earth frequently, developed systems that depended on wood and wood's flexibility. From keyed joinery at the base of the column to ascending cross bracing, the wooden structure responded to the complex challenges of potential earthquakes. Kerala has few earthquakes and builders could feel secure setting the roof structure on masonry walls. Earthquakes in Sumatra and Java have damaged many newer buildings of concrete and/or brick. The timber mosques have proven more resilient.

Roof rafters were frequently extended for overhangs to shade the walls and protect the surfaces, especially the woodcarvings, from the monsoon rains. Eave boards and rafter tails repeated standard carved details. Hipped roofs (most commonly seen in Kerala) often had a gable set near the ridge; gable inserts displayed an array of floral and shaped carvings that also

served as ventilation panels. Gable ends often flowered into balconies, similar to those seen in palaces, with ever-finer levels of craftsmanship. The single Kerala balcony offset the symmetry of the structure but did mark the entrance to the mosque. Except for the original rectangular Malabar mosques, there is a pronounced dominance of the square plan for the prayer hall. The Indonesian tiered pyramidal roof followed the square floor plan with carved wooden panels between tiers. A system of radiating rafters framed the tapered roofs. The mosques had an ensemble of roofs, often at different slopes, but a sense of balance and proportion prevailed.

Throughout South and Southeast Asia carved panels are a constant. Utilized at gable ends, at openings and at clerestories their value at increasing ventilation flow has proven positive over centuries. For roofing, early mosques employed thatch. In Kerala the well-endowed mosque had copper shingles applied over a wood base. By the 16th century, clay tiles had replaced palm thatch in India. *Ijuk* was the roofing material par excellence of Indonesia. Coming from the palm tree native to the archipelago, *ijuk* historically roofed all the buildings of Indonesia. Zinc-coated metal roofing, brought by the Dutch colonialists, became ubiquitous throughout Indonesia and only a few mosques in Sumatra and some village mosques in Java maintain thatch roofs.

The crown of the Indonesian roof is called the *mustaka*. This rooftop ornament finishes off the composition and can be made of clay or metal. It is found throughout Java, in some Sumatran mosques and even in Kerala. Since none of the original monsoon mosques had minarets, this marker of the high point was a symbolic finale to the ensemble. In Indonesia, the land of volcanoes, the roof form and the peak of the mosque mimic the old sacred mountains. When looking over the agricultural landscape of palms and rice fields, it is only the mosque 'peak' that stands above all.

There are always facilities for the ablutions obligatory before prayer. Even if one is not going to pray, the feet must be washed before entering the mosque. The washing area differs in every culture, from the fountains of the Middle East to a simple rectangular bath. In steamy Kerala and Indonesia, the fountain was transformed into a pool; water was plentiful and washing a pleasurable and favoured activity. Most tropical Asians could easily connect the act of washing with prayer, as Hinduism has a tradition of ceremonial bathing. For the Malayalees, the ablution pool was placed in an open veranda or an attached structure. Several mosques housed the pool in a two-storey tower adjacent to the main building. Some adopted the courtyard tradition;

Ablution pool, Kerala

the open-air pool fills the courtyard space while a four-sided surround provides a roofed enclosure. In Java and Sumatra, the pool is typically outside, adjacent to the mosque, serving as fish farm, washing centre, bathing area for the community and water storage for the ever-present rice fields. The Javanese mosque compound often included a moat-like water feature around the mosque that served as a marker in the passage from public street to private prayer. The grand water elements are a reminder of another time and as mosques modernize, they are disappearing. Community members now bathe at home. The participants at Friday prayer no longer wish to bend down to wash and they don't want to use a common pool. Stand up fountains and individual water taps are replacing the spacious, evocative pools.

Popular imagery equates a mosque with domes and minarets. Neither dome nor minaret has a liturgical imperative and neither was present in the vernacular of the Malabar Coast or Indonesia. People believed that the height of structures should be kept below the tops of coconut palms. Tropical landscapes were marked by one- and two-storied houses, villages with gardens. Roof construction was of wood, not stone. The minaret developed in the crowded city, but in villages the call to prayer could easily reach the people. The muezzin would climb up to the roof or the second floor. The Malay-Indonesian world had a tradition of a drum call which was transformed into a call for prayer. Now, of course, there are loudspeakers perched on every mosque's roof, but the majority of the Indonesian mosques hold a place of honour

Country mosque in Java where an expanded moat has been taken over for the day by young swimmers.

for their ancient drum (*bedug* or *beduk*). A *bedug* can be huge, a giant circular drum, and is often joined by a hanging log drum, both hewn from a single tree. The finishing touch on many drums is a top crafted from the leather of the much-loved water buffalo. Hung either horizontally or vertically, the double-barrelled drum comes out of the Indonesian *gamelan* tradition.

As in the case of the *bedug*, the Islam that came from the Middle East was adapted by the Muslims of South and Southeast Asia (children or grandchildren of converts). They built their mosques using local designs and craftsmen. Today, mosques are being torn down to be replaced by awkward copies of modern Arabic mosques or throwbacks to Mughal designs. "…confidence in the value of local traditions has now sadly been lost, and not only in South India but also in Southeast Asia buildings of little architectural merit, imitating in concrete domed and arched forms, and minarets, are sprouting up." (Shokoohy 2003, 132) While the mosque building is not considered sacred, the human and spiritual energy that went into the construction cannot be disregarded. It is sadly ironic that after five hundred years of mosque-building the local style is being discarded for an import. The lovingly crafted and sculpted structures are being replaced with flat rough concrete; openness to sea breezes swapped for sealed spaces.

The grandeur of the old halls with their outstanding craftsmanship and powerful spatial presence is missing in the new mosques which rely on bigness and marble for impact. How different are these mosques that have entrances

A classic *bedug* (drum) pair, Java

of tall arched walls and then proceed to push one down to a low-ceilinged prayer hall? And the 'remodels' of the old are even more painful; the soaring ceilings have been flattened and lowered. Do the mosque authorities only want you to bow down to the floor, never uplifted by the space? Throughout the monsoon zone, one often sees a man or woman enter an old mosque and just stand for a moment in awe at the calm and beauty of the space. They look up to offer a prayer before the usual prostration on the floor. The monsoon mosques are cubic but their essence (even in Kerala) is vertical. One is uplifted to soar to the crowning roof.

The story of the creation of an indigenous mosque architecture provides a valuable historical example of cultural adaptation. Globally, there are few extant reminders of this decidedly non-violent process. Through the forces of nature, economics and fundamentalism, the tropical mosques are rapidly disappearing. The wooden structures described in this book are some of the few survivors.

India: Malabar

Malabar map, 1616 Jodocus Hondius

"In the kingdom of Malabar there are many other foreign Moors as well in the town of Calicut, who are called Pardesis, Arabs, Persians, Gujeratis. ... As the trade of this country is very large, they gathered here in great numbers. They sail everywhere with goods of many kinds. ... In the days of their prosperity in trade and navigation they built in the city keeled ships of a thousand..."

Duarte Barbosa (c. 1500 AD)

"The distinctive cultures of the south, shaped in large measure by their oceanic connections, are a reminder that historical cultural and political regions do not map onto the areas defined by today's nation states…The coastal areas of the south often had far closer connections via ocean routes than they did with many parts of inland India."

Metcalf 2009, 3

"And to begin with, pass the pepper……the pepper, if you please; for if it had not been for peppercorns, then what is ending now in East and West might never have begun. Pepper it was that brought Vasco da Gama's tall ships across the ocean, from Lisbon's Tower of Belem to the Malabar Coast: first to Calicut and later, for its lagoony harbour, to Cochin."

Rushdie 1995, 4

The Malabar Coast, now part of the Indian state of Kerala, has captured the imagination of travellers and geographers for centuries. In the 14th century, Ibn Battuta travelled to the area; 15th-century visitors included Ma Huan of China, Samarqandi of Persia,[1] the Italian merchant Niccolo de Conti and many more. All these visitors wrote of the presence of Muslims along the Malabar Coast. Kerala, the land of lush vegetation, extensive backwaters, ubiquitous coconut trees and universal literacy, stretches along the Arabian Sea. Isolated from the rest of India for millennia by the dense forests and mountains of the Western Ghats,[2] the people along the coastline, a thin sliver of land between mountains and sea, interacted easily with traders from around the world. The sea at Kerala's doorstep brought wealth, new religions, new ideas, traders and settlers. Early settlers included

---

1. Abd-al-Razzaq Samarqandi was an ambassador of the Persian ruler. His writings about his visit to Calicut give a unique look into mid-15th century Calicut. Ma Huan was a convert to Islam and served as a translator for Zheng He, the famous leader of the Chinese expeditions to the West. He visited Calicut twice in the mid 1440s.
2. Ghat is a multipurpose word; it signifies the mountainous range running along the spine between Kerala and Tamil Nadu and also refers to the steps along a river used by the people to descend into the river.

Hindu temple in Kochi with traditional Kerala decorated gables

Tali Temple in Kozhikode, 1901 (ASI photo). The temple remains a centre of activity today.

Middle Eastern Christians and Jews, followed later by Muslims and peoples from throughout the Indian Ocean littoral. Unfortunately, the arrival of the European Vasco da Gama in 1498 reversed centuries of a world trade where no one power had dominated. Merchants from throughout the Indian Ocean and their ancient trade networks would be forever weakened.

In the watery paradise of Kerala, a vast network of lakes, rivers and canals functions as the navigable waterways that connect countryside to the city. Until recently all the products of the region—spices, wood products, rice and bamboo—arrived by *thoni* (country boats) at the portside warehouses. Foreign goods arrived from China, Southeast Asia and, by way of Arabia, the West. Extending far back in history, there are writings about historic ports along the Arabian Sea. Roman records speak of the port of Muziris

where gold was exchanged for pepper, known for centuries as "black gold". Recently, evidence of Muziris (which became Cranganore and is now Kodungallur) has been rediscovered through archaeological excavations.[3] The Malabar Coast served as an entrepôt for the Middle East and Southeast Asia, a hinge between the western and eastern ends of the Indian Ocean, a resting place for the time between the southwest and the northeast monsoon. These winds brought ships from both the East and West. As we shall see in the following chapters, a second hinge (joining China and India) was formed at ports facing the Straits of Malacca.

Presently, both Cochin and Calicut (now Kochi and Kozhikode) have populations of over half a million. Unlike predominantly Hindu (80 per cent) India, most Kerala cities do not have a dominant faith. Kerala has been known for

---

3. For more information on the dig, see *Unearthing Pattanam*, by P.J. Cherian and Jaya Menon, the catalogue for the 2014 exhibit at the National Museum, New Delhi.

the quiet coexistence among its many religious groups. Along the coast Hindu believers make up 45–50 per cent and Muslims 25–40 per cent. Kochi has a large Christian (35 per cent) community, tracing its origins back to St Thomas the Apostle. Evidence of Jewish settlements goes back to the 1st century AD; unfortunately, in the last decades, much of the once strong Jewish population of Kerala has emigrated to Israel. In this urban potpourri, people became more open to a multicultural view of themselves, identifying with their community and not exclusively with religion. Social reforms instigated after Independence by a radicalized Kerala state government, including land ownership restructuring, health care, and schooling for all, helped to create an educated, healthy citizenry.

Faith plays a major role in Malayalee identity, but it is integrated into other aspects of life. It is to this balanced view that a new generation of Indian scholars is turning, noting the positive interplay between the different peoples of India that occurred in pre-colonial times. Instead of repeating the old tales of separation, they are looking to identities forged within the Indian culture, expanded and not bound by the forces of religion. Religions arriving in India were in fact "Indianized". Social practices of Malabar were incorporated into both Christianity and Islam.

The original Muslims of Kerala came from Gujarat, Yemen and Baghdad. Ancient travellers to the Malabar Coast noted merchants from far and wide: China, Sumatra, Bengal, Arabia, Persia and even Ethiopia. In seventh-century Cranganore the reigning ruler greeted Malik Ibn Dinar,[4] the first Islamic leader to reach his shores, with great respect. Tradition has it that Malik Ibn Dinar so impressed all with his wisdom and piety that he was allotted land for a settlement. He and his followers then built what may have been the first mosques in India.

Taking a little from the vernacular house and the temple, the Muslims created the unique graceful Kerala mosque. The tradition of working with wood was strong in Kerala. Teak and other jungle woods were intricately carved and transformed into vents, structural posts and beams, ceilings, and gable end screens. Mosques had large sloped roofs with wide overhangs; many had an elaborate entry gable, a well-known element in Kerala structures. Kerala has few of the great stone temples of Tamil Nadu and North India. Instead, craftsmen celebrated the lush and luxuriant nearby forests and the wealth of wood products: teak, bamboo, coconut, rosewood, sandalwood and more. Today, the mosques retain a memory of the skills of generations of wood artisans.

The old mosques were typically two-storeyed, although many started their lives as one-storey structures that were expanded in later centuries. Usually, one-storey verandas (or colonnades) enveloped the building to provide shaded space for discussion and/or prayer. Walls were constructed of the local laterite stone. Early mosques had interior columns, but these disappeared in the next generation of mosques. Upper floors were used for study, for visiting scholars, and for

---

4. This date is much debated. Sheikh Ahmad Zainuddin Makhdoom II (1531–1583), the 16th century author of the well-known *Tuhafat al-Mujahidin*, stated "that Islam veritably gained a foothold on the Malabar Coast only in the 9th century and later."

overflow crowds at Friday prayer. Many of the mosques repeated a smaller version of the *mihrab* upstairs. Balustered openings in the floor allowed the voice of the imam preaching below to reach the worshippers above.

The typical Kerala roof structure (with modifications) was utilized for the mosque roof. Local artisans, many of whom were Hindu, followed laid-down principles for construction. Rafters were placed to create roof trusses, with horizontal members reinforcing the composition. Radial roof rafters are found on square structures and at hipped roof ends. Jacques Dumarcay, in his many studies of traditional Asian construction, notes the consistent and unique South Indian methods for framing the great sloping roofs. We will see a version of the radiating roof framing in the square pavilions and mosques of Indonesia.

Hidden away in the trading neighbourhoods of the old port cities of Malabar sit the local mosques, tucked behind walls and courtyards. In every neighbourhood different ethnic groups and religious sects built mosques, often funded by a thriving merchant. They all used the local building technology. The greatest concentration of the old mosques can be found in Kozhikode, Ponnani (the religious centre for Islam in Kerala), and Kochi. All three of these cities sit on the Arabian Sea and have a long history of trade.

The American historian Richard White wrote about the "search for accommodation and common meaning..." People "met and regarded each other as alien, as other… over the next two centuries, they constructed a common, mutually comprehensible world." The relationship between Hindu, Christian and Muslim in Malabar was eased by the longstanding presence of traders along the Malabar Coast. This predisposed the local people to an acceptance of the "other", the alien foreigner.

Much of the current debate about the clash between Muslim and non-Muslim cultures has been concerned about the role of violence. Highlighting the indigenous Kerala mosque architecture provides a valuable historical example of cultural adaptation. In today's polarized world, there is much to be gained by showcasing enlightened prototypes that are a reminder of the longstanding peaceful assimilation of Islam into the life of Kerala.

Calicut/Kozhikode

On the north Kerala coast, Kozhikode, known as the "City of Spices", controlled the trade of black pepper and cardamom, along with a large trade in soft cotton fabrics, known as "calico". The cloth originated in Kozhikode (then known as Calicut) in the 11th century. Dyed, printed and sold as "calico prints", this product was immensely popular and caused such grief to the British wool market that for a time the British banned the sale of this cloth in Great Britain.

Ibn Battuta arrived in Kozhikode around 1341 and noted an "atmosphere of peaceful coexistence and mutual tolerance between Hindus and Muslims..." The arrival of Vasco da Gama's ship one hundred and fifty-seven years later was not a good day for the fortunes of Kozhikode. The Zamorin (King of the Kingdom of Kozhikode) faced a continual battle with Europeans in order to maintain his dominance. Although the Zamorin was a Hindu, he protected the local merchants of all faiths and would not cede supremacy to the Europeans.

Large family homes (*tharavadu*) in the neighbourhood around Mithqal Palli; the mosque roof can be seen at upper right.

The impressive pool that centres the Kuttichira neighbourhood, Kozhikode

Eventually Kochi, with a better-positioned port, overshadowed Kozhikode and the city we see today is a shadow of its former glory.

"Once the Portuguese channeled most of the trade to the ports of Cochin and Goa over which they [the Portuguese] exercised exclusive control, the remaining ports of India were reduced to secondary stature contingent on Portuguese sufferance. By the eighteenth century, an English visitor described Calicut as a modest fishing village of low leaf-thatched huts, although it was still the primary metropolis of Malabar in which remnants of the Indianized Muslim merchant community continued to exploit a dying trade, albeit under the heels of European hegemony". (Abu Lughod 1989, 276)

Kuttichira is the area granted by the Zamorin (or Samutiri/Samoothiri) to the trading community sometime in the 13th century. Bordered by the Arabian Sea to the west, the Kallai River to the south, and a trading street to the north, the area evolved into a Muslim settlement. The river

Mithqal Mosque

brought timber and spices down from the Ghats. Big Bazaar Road became the headquarters of the spice and grain trade, and the Sea carried all the goods to foreign lands. To the northeast a large tank marks the heart of the ancient city. Where once sat the ruler's palace, there is now a Vedic college (known as the Zamorin's college) and the main Hindu temple. A visit to the temple (Kozhikode Tali Temple) provides an observer with an excellent example of the Kerala vernacular and a look at many elements that would reappear in the Malabar mosques.

Narrow lanes radiate out from the great tank of Kuttichira (*chira* means tank, the typical large water body that is the focus of South Indian towns). Kuttichira is a particularly unique community in that it is part of the zone of northern Kerala that follows a matrilineal system. Besides a series of impressive mosques, a central 1.5 acre pond, and a historic market area, Kuttichira holds a wealth of large family homes. These *tharavadu* (*tarawad*) are ancestral joint household homes where families live communally. The groupings of *tharavadu* present a powerful urban element. The large multi-family houses are a physical response to a matrilineal system where houses pass from mothers to daughters. Daughters stay at their mother's house and new husbands move into their wife's mother's family home. When a marriage occurs, a new room is set up in the daughter's family home for the newlyweds. There are approximately five hundred *tharavadu* in Kuttichira.

Typically, the homes are rambling two-storey gable-roofed structures constructed of laterite, a local stone whose properties allow walls to breathe. Locals claim that laterite stone pulls coolness from the earth and exhales it into the building. The houses have interior courtyards, wooden upper floors and ceilings, and decorative carving of wood components. Most of the houses have a front veranda with a *kottil* (raised platform) for meeting visitors. Air circulation in and around the building is ensured by a walled outdoor space, shaded by mango, coconut, jackfruit and other native trees. The entire composition provides cool interior spaces. A roofed gate at the street marks the entry.

All of these elements are typical of north Kerala. Both Nair Hindus and Mappila Muslims follow long-established matrilineal customs. The Mappila Muslims and Koyas (respected persons) of today are descendants of Malayalees who converted to Islam, some marrying Arabs. Since many of these local converts were from the Nair community, which followed the matrilineal tradition, joint family homes continued.

Haunting the alleys of Kuttichira is the sense that it is all about to disappear. There are already many new concrete houses inserted amidst the wooden-shuttered, plastered-walled and timber-roofed mansions. The old houses of stone and timber, plaster and clay tile are being replaced by concrete flat-roofed rectangular 'boxes'. An article in the *New York Times* (Romig, 1 March 2017) reports:

> "…concrete is cheap, strong, easy to use and highly versatile. In part it's cultural: Building a house out of brawny concrete has come to be viewed by many as a matter of prestige. "They feel that beauty is a beast," the architect B.R. Ajit told me ruefully. The law encourages this tendency. One environmental lawyer explained to me that the Indian building code recognizes a house as a house only if it's made from specific heavy materials — concrete included."

Prayer hall, Mithqal Palli

Mithqal Palli[5] (Mithqal Mosque) is the most prominent mosque of Kuttichira. The mosque centres the community, reflecting onto the grand pond/tank. Mehrdad Shokoohy designated the mosque "among the major monuments of Muslim India." (Shokoohy 2003, 153) Built by Nakhuda Mithqal,[6] a famous 14th-century merchant and ship owner, the mosque was standing in 1341 when Ibn Battuta, the traveller/chronicler extraordinaire, visited Kozhikode. Mithqal has undergone many re-buildings, but the form and the majesty of the many-tiered roof and the raised stone base all respect the original structure, a direct descendent of Kerala palace and temple vernacular. The series of arched openings that form the mosque walls create a permeable flow of air and people.

The rectangular mosque has four tiers of sloped roofs with louvered canted walls between the top two floors and an open walkway circumnavigating the second floor. Although the structure is

5. 'Palli' is the Malayalam word for mosque or church. 'Mithqal' is also written as 'Mishkal'.
6. 'Nakhuda' is the Persian word for the captain of the ship. Mithqal had strong ties with Yemen and some state that he was born in Yemen.

Exterior of Mithqal Palli

rectangular, the prayer hall is a square. The ground floor prayer hall has an open corridor on three sides and an antechamber in the east (opposite from the west-facing *mihrab*). The structure is timber, except for the ground floor walls which are laterite stone set on a raised plinth of local granite. Rows of carved wood pillars repeat motifs of traditional Kerala columns. As the column rises the shape transforms back and forth, from square to octagon. We shall see this same motif in several other early mosques. Wooden ceilings, a feature in the early Kerala mosques, highlight the structural system of large timber beams supporting smaller floor joists.

A covered ablution pool was added to the northeast, sometime in the 17th century. It is believed that the large stone trough in the middle of the pool was originally outdoors and served for ablution. Investigations of these early Kerala mosques reveal that interior pools are additions.

Early mosques had wash areas outside, only later were these incorporated into the structure.

Everyone agrees that Mithqal was attacked and burned in 1510 by the Portuguese. Supposedly the adjacent Jami Masjid was not attacked, probably because it was smaller, less grand and not as prominent a presence. Locals state that Mithqal had seven roofs before the attack, but when it was reconstructed in 1578–9, the congregation settled for the present four floors.

Wood is on the one hand vulnerable, but on the other, a repairable and replaceable material. The mosque's present integrity, despite centuries of change, reflects a strong community pride of place. The layers are a history of Kozhikode and the many inscriptions throughout the mosque are an encyclopaedia of the influences felt by this seaport community.

Ablution pool at Mithqal Palli with the original stone trough that was used for obligatory washing.

The signboard in front of the Mithqal Mosque in Kozhikode states:

> "The mosque, where a number of students, scholars, historians and research student including foreigners are visiting, was also a place for stay and study to the Muslim scholars in ancient times."

Unfortunately, this open invitation is no longer followed. Women and non-Muslim are not allowed entry, a practice followed at some Kerala mosques. Sadly, at the local Hindu temple just down the road only Hindus are allowed. On the other hand, throughout much of India and all of Malaysia and Indonesia entry into the mosque is open to all, as in many religious buildings worldwide.

Today, the Mithqal Mosque stands tall and elegant, the honoured recipient of a 2011–12 renovation. Paint was removed from all the teak columns on the main floor and replaced with a clear finish. Of the multitude of columns (twenty-four), about ten were replaced with new teak timbers. Some roof work was done, including the repair of roof timbers. The exterior was re-plastered and painted. New corner supports were built at the upper roof section.

The present Qazi[7] states that funding for the restoration was from the local community. In fact, ONGC (Oil and Natural Gas Corporation Ltd.) funded two projects: one at the nearby Tali Temple and one the Mithqal Mosque.[8] Both are historic properties and the grants ensure that these buildings will continue to enlighten and serve the community into the future. Grants such as these are extremely rare. This one occurred despite the religious connection (ONGC, being a public entity, had to receive a waiver to apply the funds). The projects happened because an influential patron/politician pushed them forward. The majority of the historic mosques of the Malabar Coast have no enlightened benefactor.

Jami Masjid is an extended and enlarged version of the original smaller mosque which dates to the 14th century. Arabic inscriptions can be found carved on the wooden lintels of the mosque antechamber. The oldest is from 1480 and refers to a need for restoration of the mosque, implying that the mosque was already old. This mosque is within hailing distance of Mithqal, sited directly on the edge of a lane in the midst of the great *tharavadu* houses.

---

7. The Qazi (Khazi) or Qadi was originally the appointed judge for a Muslim community. Today, the term usually refers to a mosque administrator.
8. See "Mishkal: A Mosque that withstood centuries". *Malayalam*, 6-19-2011 and Amitav Rajan "PSU bends rules to fund temple and mosque to keep PMO happy." *The Indian Express*, 9-9-2008.

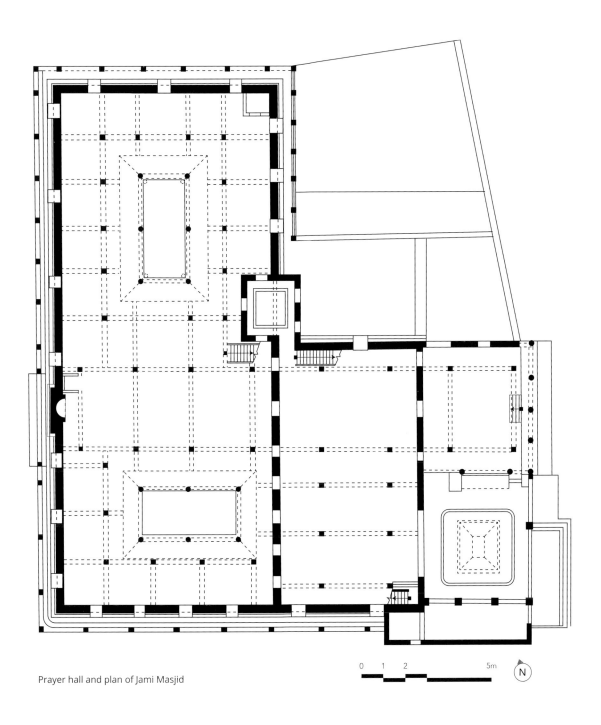

Prayer hall and plan of Jami Masjid

0   1   2   5m   N

Exterior of Jami Masjid. Original mosque on the left, with 17th-century additions to its right.

The main entry, complete with a classic Kerala carved gable, faces east towards the lane. The entry ceiling displays a richly carved coffered ceiling with lotus and floral designs and a series of Arabic inscriptions. South of the entrance sits a newer ablution chamber. Moving towards the prayer hall and passing through the large antechamber, a second, older smaller pool can be found adjacent to the main rectangular prayer hall. The mosque forms an 'L', with an expanded prayer hall opening to the north. The two-storey mosque has a series of interior open courtyards creating an eclectic mix of roof slopes in addition to open pools that collect water and boost ventilation. This combination of open courtyards and surrounding structure is common in Kerala courtyard homes.[9] Exterior columns and a colonnade run around the south, west, and a portion of the north and east.

The Jami is an excellent example of sympathetic remodels. The 17th century additions join to the original at a complimentary scale and reflect the growing community of believers. Unlike the garish additions we will see elsewhere, the Jami offers a comforting series of spaces. A more recent series of renovations replaced outside wood with Irul—a moisture resistant wood. Inside columns were replaced with teak. The exterior columns at the

---

9. For more on the traditional courtyard house (*nalukettu*s), see Thampuran, 2001. The book also has valuable information on the other traditional home of Malabar, which is similar to the *tharavadu*.

Prayer hall, with one of the interior courtyards visible on the right, Jami Masjid

The entry hall at Muchundi Palli. The ceiling is original but columns have been covered.

colonnade are now steel pipes with concrete bases that may be attempts to imitate an original plinth.

Muchundi Palli is the next old mosque, moving south down the lane from the Jami Masjid. The mosque has granite tablets describing the gift of property from a 13th century Zamorin. Locals believe that the garden to the north of the mosque was land given by the Zamorin to ensure that the mosque was always kept alive and funded. The mosque has a connection to Zainuddin Makhdoom II, the author of *Tuhafat al-Mujahidin*,[10] who taught at the mosque in the 16th century.

The title of 'oldest' mosque may belong to Muchundi, although each source appears to have different dates for the mosques.[11] The rectangular three-storey mosque has a similar layout as the Jami with an entry hall leading to an antechamber and then the prayer hall. However, there are no colonnades. The ablution chamber sits to the north of the antechamber. Ceiling coffering at the entry closely matches that of Jami Masjid, as do a series of carved inscriptions in Arabic and Tamil.

Muchundi has had several of its louvered upper walls covered, but one would hope that it could be restored to its former grandeur. The interior has also suffered from recent remodels, including the addition of marble slabs to wooden columns.

These three mosques tell not only the history of the Muslim community but also the story of the creation of a vernacular form and provide a glimpse at life before the arrival of the Europeans. Although actual construction dates are impossible to verify, the mosques hold a wealth of stories. Inscriptions cite many builders and a plethora of

10. The book chronicles the devastation inflicted by the Portuguese and is an excellent history of South Indian Muslims.
11. See Shokoohy, 2003, and Kasthurba, 2012.

dates. Carved boards give dates for re-buildings, clarifying that all three were constructed before the arrival of Vasco da Gama and the wave of European colonialists.

Cochin/Kochi

Moving south along the coast, we reach Kochi, another jewel of the trading culture. Kochi gained ascendancy after the great flood of 1341 silted up the historic port of nearby Cranganore (once Muziris). Kochi is sited on a peninsula, with the Arabian Sea to the west, a sheltered waterway and port to the east and the river channel's opening to the sea to the north. The natural harbour connected inland backwaters and global sea lanes, offering a protected landing for generations of overseas traders and local merchants. After Vasco da Gama was thrown out of the northern Kerala port of Kozhikode by the powerful Zamorin, the Portuguese looked to Kochi. Thus began four hundred and fifty years of European interference and eventual domination. Fort Cochin (at the northern tip of the peninsula) became the first European settlement in India, and one of the few with a history of Portuguese, Dutch and English presence. The adjacent older settlement, also called Mattancherry, remained the home of the ruling maharaja and site of the port. Here the storage, shipping, and trading of goods took place. As in other colonial port gateways, a multi-ethnic population learned to live and work together.

Today, a new port across from peninsular Kochi has become the centre of modern shipping. In the old city, the ancient commodities of rice and spices move to a different pace, at reduced volume, in and out of decaying godowns on the heads of porters. The newest 'goods' are tourists, arriving by cruise ship, airplane, train and backwater boat.

South of the old Maharaja's estate and Jewtown (once home to Jewish merchants) sits Kochangadi, the original Muslim quarter of Kochi. Stretching along the backwaters to the east, far from the eyes of the European colonialists who rarely travelled to Mattancherry and now far from the tours of cruise passengers and assorted tourists, this area has been home to Muslims since the founding of the city. The settlers chose the unoccupied east side of the peninsula for its excellent harbour. Here they were protected from the rough open seas to the west. The life of the local Muslims, complete with schools, mosques, shops, storehouses, homes and shrines thrived. Today, the population remains and the five daily calls to prayer continue to fill the air, distinct voices emanating from the many different mosques.

Successful merchants built fine homes in Kochangadi and contributed to the construction of its mosques. The neighbourhood has more than a dozen mosques, catering to a predominantly Sunni population, with a variety of sub-sects and ethnic backgrounds. Coconut palms sway overhead, lush vegetation shades narrow roads, large water reservoirs bring to mind the classic Indian temple pool. Streets jog, lanes branch off the main roadway, twisting and turning to reach groups of family homes. There are few cars on these back lanes and a village atmosphere permeates the neighbourhood. Children are everywhere, women gather to cook, to wash clothes, to talk, and to watch their offspring.

The neighbourhood is dotted with shrines dedicated to the early scholars who brought Islam to Kochi. Many are secreted in medieval lanes. One node holds the grave of Ali Marankar, a personage who residents confess they know little of except for the remembered name. An ancient banyan tree has embraced the tomb and the remnants of the shrine's stone walls.

This neighbourhood was once graced by fine old family homes like those found in Kuttichira, but in recent years old homes have been torn down, to be replaced by concrete masses, what the locals call "Gulf mansions". Many of the young men of Kochangadi work in the Persian Gulf, and when they come home they feel they must have a residence of marble and glass. These workers also fund new mosques. Returning dollars and rupees carry with them the aesthetic of Gulf modernism (and a less tolerant Islam). Modern architecture that is all glitz with no connection to the place is seen as ideal. The new flat-roofed concrete structures try to ignore the monsoons, the heat, and the local traditions.

Chembitta Palli

The heart of Kochangadi is Chembitta Palli, the oldest and finest mosque of the area. Built after Mithqal Palli in Kozhikode and connected to that community by Islamic leaders, Chembitta Palli displays many similarities with the senior mosques to the north.

Coffered ceiling and prayer hall entry at Chembitta Palli

The grand two-storey mosque is centrally located on a large plot of land. Well-travelled paths pass through the low-walled compound, connecting roads to the east, west and south. Sharing the compound with the regal mosque building are two shrines and several outbuildings. The heavily vegetated ground is predominantly used for burial. Graveyards to the north and south of the mosque

have a scattering of old granite and new marble headstones. Most graves are merely body length mounds that slowly settle back into the earth.

Sometime between 1520 and 1540 the mosque that is seen today was built (or rebuilt after the Portuguese burned down the original). Inscriptions date the mosque 'rebuilding' at 926 AH (1520 AD).[12] Whether it was built new or built

12. Islamic years are counted from the date of the *hijra* (the Prophet's journey from Makkah to Medina), July 622 AD. Hijra dates will be shown with AH.

Exterior of Chembitta Palli; new two-storey additions can be seen to the left.

on the foundation of a smaller mosque is up for discussion. A driving force at the mosque was the scholarly family of Sayyid Bukhari. His grave and that of a descendant are located in a three-chambered shrine north of the mosque. The shrine is a variant of the Kerala 'house', constructed of stone walls topped by two hipped roofs with carved gable boards.

Stories abound about the Bukhari clan. The chief figure was Sayyid[13] Ismail Bukhari, a spiritual leader of the community. The Bukhari clan may have originally come from Bukhara (in central Asia), but residency on Kavaratti Island of Lakshadweep and in Kannur (an ancient trading port in northern Kerala) is also mentioned. The

Sayyids (many of whom were Sufi scholars) played an important part in the teaching and conversion of Muslims in Kerala, integrating local influences and encouraging cooperation with Hindus.

Chembitta Palli is a clear visual example of this assimilation. Elements adopted from Kerala houses and temples define the architecture of the mosque. Known carvers and artisans were brought from nearby areas to help build the new mosque. Records at the mosque also mention boat builders, who were well versed in woodworking. In order to position and join the sizeable beams and columns of Chembitta Palli, a knowledge and skill in working with large timbers would have been essential.

13. A Sayyid was said to be a descendent of the Prophet, but Sayyid can also be a term of respect.

Detail of the magnificent carved gable, now hidden by additions

The imams of the mosque have always told the story that has been passed down from one generation to the next about the timber that was used for the mosque: A local Jewish merchant was so impressed with the knowledge of the Sayyid that he wanted to help in the building of the mosque. He donated all the timbers. Some embroider this story by telling how the Jewish merchant then decided to convert after hearing the erudition of the Sayyid's sermon on Moses.

The second floor structure, the two-tiered roof structure and all of the columns are wood. Impressive main floor columns support the beams for the upper floor and carry the load of the roof structure to the ground. At the second floor, the columns extend up to the beams and rafters of the high roof. All of the wooden superstructure elements are notched to fit together tightly. Each column has been shaped from a single timber into alternating geometrical sections (square and octagonal), a common motif seen in Kozhikode and the wood pillars of Kerala palaces as well as the stone columns of South Indian temples.

The structure sits on a raised plinth of granite, with plastered laterite walls. From a utilitarian foundation, the building rises up, each level bringing forth more finely wrought details. An original colonnade encircled three sides. It was later enclosed with a series of rectangular shuttered openings which aligned with the interior openings, thus maintaining the light and airy feel of the interior. Inside the colonnade and at the space between interior columns and the original outside wall, the sloping rafters of the lower roof can be seen.

A gracious large entrance porch fronts the main prayer hall. Above the prayer hall doors are wood panels with carved inscriptions. The porch ceiling displays wood coffering, a device often seen in buildings of importance and found in many of the Kozhikode mosques. The structure of the entrance porch matches that of the main hall, with the sloped rafter space wrapping three sides.

The prayer hall has a single *mihrab* centred on the *qibla* (west facing) wall; this projection is not visible from the exterior because the veranda extends across this side. To the right of the *mihrab* sits the wooden *mimbar*, an excellent example of wood-carving skills of that time.

The second floor, used for study and rest, has a smaller footprint than the first as the walls align with the main floor interior columns. The space has a high open ceiling. Louvers angle outward from bottom to top (a traditional Kerala style used in palace architecture and temples and seen in all the Kozhikode mosques discussed). The upper roof of the mosque is covered with flat copper shingles (or *chembu palli*, thus the mosque name). The hipped roof has one exterior gable facing east, above the old entry. The gable takes on a balcony form with columns and balustrades, all elaborately carved in the quintessential Kerala style.

In Kochi today, there is little of such a substantial nature that dates back almost five hundred years. The building of the mosque was a major undertaking and proof of the success of the Muslim traders, their optimism, and their commitment to their community. Wealthy traders contributed funds while less affluent members of the community donated their own labour to the building project.

During Friday prayer, attendees overflow the original hall. Because of this, in recent times several concrete flat-roofed halls have been built along with a large ablution pool. An older two-storey annex, north of the main hall, houses an earlier smaller pool. The additions now extend around two sides of the old mosque and have gone from one storey to two. The long, tree-lined path from the east (and the port) now runs into an awkward concrete structure with, to add insult to injury, a fake Kerala roof. One could ask why the designers of today are not as adept as the renovators of Kozhikode's Jami Masjid. The integration of forms and alertness to materials that are seen at the Jami Masjid are missing at Chembitta Palli.

The mosque administrators have a peculiar idea of how to maintain their mosque. They have placed two large additions in positions that overpower the old mosque. All views of the once-regal carved entry facade have been obscured. Lime plaster on the laterite block walls has been replaced with cement plaster. There appears to be little understanding of the damage to old structures instigated by application of modern plastic paints and cement plaster, both impervious materials. These products do not allow the laterite walls to breathe. The loss of breathability causes dampness to accumulate in walls and migrate to the timber members, producing rot and a slow deterioration of the wood structure. Several young men of the mosque voiced objections to the renovation techniques and they were banished. Because there are no standards or controls on most of Kochi's heritage buildings, no conservation architect or city administrator has put forth an opinion. Instead of welcoming the assistance of professionals, the administrators see it as a taking of their religious freedom.

Besides these political social problems, there is a lack of knowledgeable artisans. All the wooden columns, beams and rafters of the mosque were put together without nails, with mortise and tenon joints. Present-day carpenters have lost the ability to fashion nail-less joinery for large timbers. The route that the leaders of Chembitta Palli have followed is typical of many of the Malabar mosques. Disparate materials and disproportionate massing abound. Just down the road, the Calvathy Mosque was renovated with domes and an addition that overpowers the original prayer hall. The so-called 'first' mosque of India, in nearby Kodungallur, was clad in concrete, completely covering the original structure. At least these original mosques can still be found, versus the many that have been demolished. Another mosque in Kochangadi (Akathe Palli, along with the tomb of a cherished spiritual leader[14]) was present in the 1990s and now has been completely rebuilt in another style. The shrine remains but its distinctive wooden gables were sold off.

Mammu Surka is an example of the evolution to a simpler Kerala mosque, reflecting the loss of the great fortunes of earlier times. This style of mosque was repeated up and down the Malabar Coast for centuries. Having undergone no alterations, its integrity intact, Mammu Surka is an excellent example of this period.

In calling distance of the one and a half acre compound of Chembitta Palli, Mammu Surka is a prayer mosque. The congregation attends Friday prayer at Chembitta Palli. The area between the two mosques houses several large tanks similar to that of Kuttichira. Across from Chembitta Palli sits one pond, and two hundred meters north, another pool forms part of the property of the Mammu Surka mosque. Both tanks mark probable sites of ancient springs which were enlarged for community water. Both are still used for washing by local people.

Mammu Surka is reached from the street by a small lane. Like the lanes at Chembitta Palli, this walkway serves as an east–west passage. A narrow building bordering the lane has a madrasa on the second floor and shops on the lower floor. To the left, and to the right behind the madrasa building, open space is utilized for a burial ground, complete with a grove of mature mango, jackfruit and coconut trees.

The mosque was built by Mammu Surka (or Sarka), a member of the Naina family. The Naina family, privileged members of the king's court, was also connected to Chembitta Palli. Some say they served as tax officers for the Kochi raja. Inscribed over the main entry door is the name Masjid Al Hadhadi Al Alavi, the official name given to the mosque by the builder. But the name of Al Hadhadi Al Alavi, who was a famous scholar, never had common usage among the community who prayed at the mosque. The mosque remains under the care of the Naina family. Funding for

Entry to the prayer hall, Mammu Surka

---

14. The tomb houses members of the renowned Zainuddin family, also noted as leaders at Muchundi Masjid and Ponnani. See Fels, *Mosques of Cochin* for more information on mosques in Cochin.

Foot pool, Mammu Surka

the operation of the mosque comes from the rent of seven small shops on the property and the harvesting of ten coconut trees.

Construction dates for the mosque are sketchy. An agreement detailing ownership and maintenance was registered with the government in 1834. By then, the mosque had already been functioning for some time and the personage noted as Mammu Surka may have been the grandfather of the agreement maker.

Although everyone agrees that the builder was of the Naina family, stories abound about the name Mammu Surka. Some say the name comes from Mansur-ika, *ika* signifying a respected elder and Mansur a well-known ship captain. Others say that the founder was a rich businessman from Mysore: Mysore-ika.

The style and construction of the mosque date it to pre-19th century. The exterior of the structure exhibits the modest outlines of a Kerala house. The interior displays the typical planked and beamed ceiling. Columns have disappeared from the prayer hall interior. Rectangular doors and shutters are of plain wooden construction. Door frames repeat the classic detail of Kerala columns: squared off edge alternating with angled edge (source of the octagon-shaped column). The two-storey prayer hall has a hipped terra cotta roof, balanced by the one-storey veranda roof. The veranda wraps all four sides of the building. A single-storey ablution area completes the composition. Recently, the terra cotta roofing tiles on the lower roof were removed, replaced with a metal roof. Hopefully the tiles on the upper roof will remain. Terra cotta is still available and is a much more appropriate roofing material for this old mosque.

Ponnani

Along the coast between Kozhikode and Kochi sits Ponnani, known as the "Makkah of Malabar". The city of Ponnani is the centre of Islamic study for the state of Kerala and was once a part of the Kingdom of Kozhikode. Here many old mosques still stand, although several have been engulfed by additions. In the 16th century, the Muslims of Malabar looked to the scholars of Ponnani for religious counsel.

Up and down the Malabar Coast traders made connections, families intermarried, and Islam spread. While each mosque has its unique history, all of the mosques display the shared traditions of wood and stone construction and a commonality of form and massing derived from the religious need for communal prayer.

Ponnani, a Malabar port city inhabited since the first century AD, was a religious centre of temples and mosques. Here can be found an ancient mosque, Thottungal Palli (or Kadavu Palli[15]). Some believe that its founding can be linked with Malik Ibn Dinar, who built ten mosques in the Cranganore/Kodungallur area (around 628 AD). Others put the 628 date as much too early and state that Thottungal Palli was built in 1200 by Shaikh Fareedhudheen and his student, Shaikh Hussein. Since Shaikh Hussein's tomb is located at the mosque, this claim may have more validity. All agree that Thottungal was the main mosque of the town until the big Jami Masjid was built in the early 1500s. Considering the long role in history of Thottungal Palli, it is all the sadder that both it and Malik Ibn Dinar's mosque at Cranganore have been encased in concrete additions. In 2008 construction was underway at Thottungal Palli; all of the verandas were gone, replaced by flat-roofed extensions, and a dome was being built at the waterside. The main prayer hall and entry remain. Both are simple open rooms with no interior columns. The structure and form indicate the beginning of the Kerala mosque style. The roof and balcony gable also remain, complete with a fantasy of decorations.

Not far from Thottungal stands the Jami Masjid of Ponnani. Construction of the mosque began sometime between 1510 and 1519 and was completed before the death in 1522 of Shaikh Zainuddin Makhdum Abu Yahya, the founder of the mosque. Called Zainuddin I, the Shaikh was the grandson of Shaikh Zainuddin (Zainudheen), the patriarch of the Zainuddin clan who is buried in Kochi. Zainuddin I, born in Kochi in 1467, was an influential man in the Kerala Islamic community. Besides founding many mosques in Ponnani he also wrote religious treatises, some of which are still used. He is buried in a tomb adjacent to the mosque entry. The Zainuddin clan was extensive, and continues today.[16] They left their mark on the port cities up and down the Kerala coast. The original Zainuddin came from Yemen, the Hadhramaut, which could be considered the origin of the Islamic community of Malabar. Another well-known Zainuddin wrote *Tuhafat al-Mujahidin* (1583), an important recounting of the South Indian Muslims. He was connected to the Muchundi Mosque in Kozhikode.

Although begun in the same period as Kochi's Chembitta Palli, the Jami Masjid of Ponnani differs in several ways. Instead of the interior wooden columns of Chembitta Palli, the Ponnani prayer hall has a series of majestic arches coming down to stone columns. Both mosques have gable porches, but the one at Ponnani is more elaborate than Chembitta Palli's. The second floor at Ponnani is a full floor with a third-floor attic above (similar to Mithqal Palli) and all floor heights are greater than Chembitta Palli. There is also disagreement about the date of the Jami Masjid that we see today. The 16th-century original (which historical documents cite as 'ninety feet long and sixty feet wide'—as it is today) was renovated in 1753–4, when it may have been expanded upward with a more elaborate gable balcony and attic. Some records indicate that the mosque was burned by the Portuguese in 1550—although the extent of the damage is not

15. *Thode* is Malayalam for canal side; *kadavu* means jetty. A canal used to connect the mosque to the river, but the river moved and is now directly at the mosque's feet.
16. The title of Makhdum was conferred on descendants of Zainuddin. The present Makhdum is the fortieth and is officially the keeper of the Jami Masjid in Ponnani.

clear. Similarities between all of these mosques include large gracious and decorated entry halls with coffered ceilings, finely carved wooden *mimbar*s, handsome inscription boards and colonnades. They all also share unsympathetic additions at the gable end. At Ponnani, a clutter of additions shields the great front. Each one has a different style (an Arabic turret, a Kerala gable, Middle Eastern mini-domes and modern cement curlicues), each one uses different materials, and sadly, each one further cuts off the view of the majestic entrance.

Fourteenth-century mosques like Kozhikode's Mithqal Palli and 16th-century mosques like Ponnani's Jami Masjid and Chembitta Palli are manifestations of the power, wealth and prestige that resided in the community. The fantastic displays of the 16th-century mosques were to be the last. The Portuguese efforts at destruction of the Muslims' trade dominance and their faith led to a humbler design, as seen at Mammu Surka. According to legend, several mosques were burned to the ground. Zainuddin I was a force who reinvigorated the population, rebuilding mosques, writing religious treatises, penning freedom songs and encouraging the Muslims to continue in their faith.

The mosques of Kerala have survived and served the local Muslim population for centuries. They are now terribly endangered, often from lack of maintenance, but more seriously threatened by the desire to build copycat Arab-style mosques. Returning home from working in the Gulf states, many Kerala Muslims wish to show gratitude for their new wealth. Because the old mosques have not received deserved recognition, the funds are often used for building a modern new mosque. To make way for the new, much larger buildings,

Expansive exterior gables and balconies, Ponnani Jami Masjid

the old mosques are demolished. Charles Correa speaks of the power of the mythic image of Islam coming from the desert:

> "For most people, these are the images of Islamic architecture that spring to the mind. Yet, ironically enough, the majority of Muslims do not live in that hot-dry belt from Algiers to Delhi, where this kind of built-form is prevalent. The vast majority … live in hot, humid climates. What they need is not dense massing, but light, free-standing built-form, and cross ventilation." (Correa 2012, 65)

The mosques of the past with open verandas, high roofs and naturally cooled interiors have been replaced with concrete domes, minarets,

Entrance hall, Ponnani Jami Masjid

Disney-ized versions of the *Arabian Nights* and Mughal monuments. The peaceful interiors with the sea breeze blowing through the opened walls are disappearing; instead air-conditioned marble palaces offer a cold hard surface for prayer.

Alerting the community to the power and beauty of the indigenous mosques is a way to acknowledge and honour their historical importance. This is the essential first step for ensuring the survival of the old mosques.

Malay Heartland
Sumatra and Peninsula Malaysia

*"However high the egret flies
It will still return to its pond"*

(Minangkabau saying)
Waterson 1990, 229

*"…the dense story of Indonesian Islam…The severe, fortress-type
masculinity of, in particular, mosques in Egypt and North Africa is
entirely absent. The prayer hall was full of children playing loudly,
mixing with the sounds of tropical birds. Women … were kneeling on
the floor in prayer. There were as many women in the mosque as men.
It was a real community gathering place."*

Kaplan 2010, 251

Sumatra, "island of gold" and locus of a wealth of spices, timber and gold, was a key player in the dynamics of world trade. A land of rumbling volcanoes, a plethora of rivers, and rich agricultural fields, Sumatra functioned as hinge between China and India. Geographically positioned to separate the Indian Ocean from the China Sea, the giant island became a trading nexus flanked by two powerful kingdoms. The other hinge, the coastal cities of India, especially the Malabar Coast, connected the world of Asia to the lands of Arabia and the Mediterranean.

Trade brought with it an enormous amount of cultural, physical, and social exchange, orchestrated by the ocean winds. "Southeast Asia fell under the regulating rhythm of the monsoon winds, which determined climatic and hence sailing patterns…The monsoons, … filled the sails of ships carrying commodities across a wider 'Indian Ocean' trading system." (Sutherland 2007, 29) The movement of people and goods thus became cyclical: between May and September/October southwest monsoons brought ships from India to Sumatra and Malaysia. Ships from China depended on northeast winds from November to January. At the hinges (Indonesian and Indian coastal cities), the traders waited for the winds to change and take them home. Settling, marrying, establishing long-term trade contacts, they

Late 19th century photograph of Minangkabau mosque, Sumatra

lounged in port cities for months. It has long been recognized that Islam was adopted slowly by the peoples of Indonesia and Malaysia. Conversion happened over time, through Sufi missionaries and traders, because of financial gain, marital persuasion and even as resistance to the forceful entry of Western powers. At the end of the 13th century, Marco Polo noted the existence of 'Mahometans' but labelled most of the Sumatran islanders as savages and idolaters. By the mid-14th century the well-known Muslim traveller Ibn Battuta wrote of the warm welcome he received from the prince of 'Samudra'. These travellers from the West understood little of the complex and ingenious melding of animist, Buddhist,

and Hindu beliefs into Islam. *Adat*, the richly orchestrated customs and laws of the place, was the core of island life and inevitably was integrated into the new religion.

In Sumatra the mosques were built, literally raised up, by people of the community. Unlike Java where there was royal support, Sumatra had no island-wide infrastructure of power. There is only slight mention of the Sumatran mosque in written history, including the books of Stamford Raffles and dozens of Dutch scholars, and on to volumes by anthropologists, sociologists, and historians. Regarding the Minangkabau of central Sumatra, writers focused on an examination of the matrilineal society and the long houses. Many spoke of how Islam was integrated into an existing system. But they neglected to look at or discuss the vernacular mosque. In Jeffrey Hadler's excellent book[1] on the Minangkabau society, two photos have mosques in the background, but his study was focused on the village structure. The story of the creation of a variant on the local vernacular, built by and for the people, appears to have garnered little interest.

Today, the surviving timber mosques built by the converts are few and far between. These raised structures, square in plan, and with a multi-tiered roof, are predominately found along the West Sumatra coast, in the agricultural highlands of the Minangkabau. A scattering of other survivors rest in Kampar, Jambi, Palembang, and Indrapuri. In West Sumatra, embraced by a series of volcanoes and lakes, the Minangkabau people have maintained their mosques. Rebuilding, restoring, and re-arranging, the local communities have sustained a vernacular. "In contrast to Western notions … repairs and replicas of weathered originals represent continuity in Minangkabau thought." (Capistrano 1997, 85) A Minangkabau proverb reads:

> "The old may be changed to renew
> The damaged should be renewed
> When it is good it should be used forever…"

Many of these elegant mosques are titled "Masjid Tua" or old mosque as a sign of respect for their age, their history and their continuing usage. Jonny Wongso, a professor at Bung Hatta University in Padang, sees the soul of a Minangkabau town in three elements: the *masjid*, *balai adat* (hall), and *rumah gadang* (the big house). Without these elements the town has no soul. They ARE Minangkabau culture. Jonny calls them the "*nagari*" elements, the core of the home-place.

The timber mosque was once ubiquitous across Sumatra and Malaysia, even extending up into southern Thailand. Photographic records display a tradition that dominated the building of mosques on both sides of the Straits of Malacca. The old photos reveal the square, two- to three-tiered roofed structures that we will examine in Western Sumatra. The local tradition of a raised timber structure was translated to the mosque. The timber roof construction of the region was adapted for a square plan. Of the mosques in the Aceh region that are documented in photographs and travellers' writings, only a few have survived. In Malaysia, even fewer mosques remain. The two most noted are Kampung Laut mosque (1730s) near Kota Bharu and Malacca's Masjid Kampung Hulu (1728).[2]

Many think "that the two great cultures of the archipelago are the Javanese and the Minangkabau." (Hadler 2008, 1) The people of the Minangkabau region played an outsized role in the history of Indonesia. Yet, they have constituted only a small percentage of the country's population.

---

1. Hadler, Jeffrey. *Muslims and Matriarchs.*
2. Malaysian mosques utilized a typology strikingly similar to that of Sumatra. The Malay people lived in Sumatra and Malaysia, two lands intimately connected through the Straits of Malacca. One view has it that 'Minangkabau was in fact the cradle land of the Malays. While about one and a half million Malays have remained in Minangkabau proper, an equal number migrated in Hindu times to Malacca and other coastal places of the archipelago.' (Edwin M. Loeb, *Sumatra, Its History and People*, Kuala Lumpur: Oxford University Press, (1935) 1972, p. 97).

We will examine the Minangkabau mosques not only because they remain a presence, but also because the Minangkabau have a unique culture and history that is visible in the mosques. In Aceh, earthquakes, colonialism and changes in religious leanings eliminated the graceful timber mosques and replaced them with domed copies of India and west Asia. In Malaysia, oil wealth and pride in a new nation drove the Malaysians to rebuild in a contemporary style.

Throughout Indonesia, the Minangkabau of the West Sumatra region are known for their adaptability. They are travellers and traders with a long tradition of migration and return.

> "…the Minangkabau, have become famous throughout the Indonesian world for their agricultural skills, for their commercial adaptability, and for their general willingness to seize new opportunities and adapt to new mental horizons, whether introduced from India, from the Middle East, or from Europe."
> (Dobbin 1983, 1)

Was it because the Minangkabau had a tradition of migration and return that they appreciated their traditional buildings? Today, the peoples of Asia often reject the traditional for the new, in the belief that modernity comes with structures of concrete and glass. The Minangkabaus have seen these modern structures, probably lived in them, and may judge them not quite so important to proving one's modernity. We can imagine that Minangkabau people appreciate, in contrast to the heat of metal and glass, the physical and cultural comforts of the raised timber post and beam structures with carved wooden air vents and sculptural roofs. Their religion and their mosque create a feeling of well-being.

As in much of Southeast Asia, the Minangkabau lived in the traditional raised house. The *rumah* (house) was a post and beam rectangular structure. Timber poles, set on stone bases (the *umpak* stone), lifted the level of the floor up several metres; walls were lightweight and breathable. Houses were raised because Sumatra is a land of marshes and rivers prone to flooding. The raised house not only protected the inhabitants from rising water and roaming animals but also provided an efficient air movement system as the cool ground air rose up through the house. The ensemble was topped by a gable roof with an extended ridge. At the roof, the Minangkabau added a unique element: a saddle-backed or horn-shaped crown that swooped, sometimes one long swoop, sometimes a series of four or six or more gables.

Each gable end is raised and descends gracefully across the middle to rise again at the opposite end, or, in a series of gables, there is only a descent from the high end to the commencement of the adjacent gable. This roof structure is called *gonjong* and can only be created by a series of slope changing rafters. What does this roof reflect? Some say it represents a boat, the prow of a ship, a bird in flight, or the horns of the much-loved water buffalo, an animal key to the life of the rice farmers. The term *gonjong* refers to the buffalo horn. The Minangkabau love for this great swoop of form can even be seen in the design of the hats of women at ceremonial gatherings. As "…the house protects the dreamer"[3], so too the regalia, especially the

---

3. Gaston Bachelard, *Poetics of Space*, 6.

Rumah gadang, a multi-family home in Payakumbuh. Multiple roof gables and carved, painted walls are distinctive elements of Minangkabau buildings.

traditional headdress of the women which reflects the protective aspects of the *gonjong* shape.

Archaeologists have found few physical remnants of early Sumatra, mainly because the people built with wood and natural fibres, which deteriorated quickly. Recent work in Muara Jambi brought to light several inscribed bricks which clearly show the raised pole structure and the winged roof.[4] These elements appear to have been around 'forever' and naturally then formed the base for the new vernacular mosque.

In highland villages, the Minangkabau created a variant of the simple *rumah*, a large, elegant multi-family home called *rumah gadang* or big house. Here the women (mothers, daughters, grandchildren) kept the family life together as the men travelled far and wide as traders and workers. West Sumatra, like the northern Kerala coast, has a matrilineal tradition of property ownership. Houses and property pass from mothers to daughters. Even where there is no *rumah gadang*, a group of smaller houses cluster together, representing an extended family. When a daughter marries, ideally a new room will be added to the *rumah gadang* or a new house built in the compound. Typically, farming villages adjoin agricultural land where rice, spices, and various food crops are tended by the villagers who prefer to live in the village and not amidst their fields. Jeffrey Hadler wrote that the story of Minangkabau culture is one of survival. "The passionately renegotiated balance between Islam and the

4. Tjoa-Bonatz, 2009

matriarchate, modernity and tradition, makes the people of West Sumatra wary of extremism and inclined to compromise." (Hadler 2008, 180)

Into this culture arrived Islam, from the port cities that thrived on the pepper trade. Sumatra is not uniformly Muslim. Different regions have embraced different faiths. The swampy river-lands that stretch north and south across the eastern part of the island were the centre of the Srivijaya, a Malay Buddhist empire that thrived from the 7th to the 12th century. Later, this entire area, along with the Malay Peninsula directly across the Straits of Malacca, became Muslim. Aceh, at the northern tip, was the landfall for Sumatra Islam. The Batak, directly to the south, remained animist or became Christian. At the heart of Sumatra, the Minangkabau converted to Islam.

> "It is hardly surprising that Islam achieved its first and most lasting successes in the Minangkabau west coast entrepots... The outer forms of Islam are easily learnt and adopted and commercial relations with the Indian traders who poured onto the coast in the heyday of the pepper trade were greatly simplified when the local brokers adopted the religion of their trading partners." (Dobbin 1983, 119)

Beginning in the late 16th century, communities began building substantial mosques. As we saw in Malabar, the structures drew from the existing pre-Islamic architectural traditions. In a creative attempt at continuity the builders appealed to local visions of 'religious'. They used traditional elements (post and beam structure, breathable lightweight walls) but instead of the

linear extended gable roof of the Sumatran house (which was rectangular), a square plan and a pyramid shaped roof were favoured. Rafters were framed in a radial pattern from peak to eave. In transforming the long gable into a pyramid, the mosque builders added horizontal open bands between the tiers of the roof to allow for ventilation and natural light. The Sumatran builders did not construct just one large roof, but three to four to five tiers of ascending roofs. What is the origin of this roof? Several authors have traced the square structure with a pyramid shaped roof to the pre-Islamic *surau*. We have no examples of this pre-Islamic structure, and can only conjecture at the transformation, but we do have still-standing Islamic *surau* from the early days of Islam in Sumatra.

> "One of the main means of Islamic penetration to the Minangkabau highlands was the *surau*, which in fact already existed before the coming of Islam. During the pre-Islamic Hindu-Buddhist period, a *surau* was used for ascetic practices and praying, and as a home for young single men. Thus, in Malay, *surau* can mean a house for praying; a dormitory where post pubescent young unmarried men lived away from the ancestral house (the dwelling place of women and children) in the matriarchal system of the Minangkabau people." (Katkova 2008)

If the *surau* theory is correct,[5] it would give another reason for the square floor plan. The oldest still standing *surau* have a square footprint. For a square structure, the pyramid shaped roof makes structural sense. In addition, the eaves are consistent on all sides. The small *surau* probably had a one-tier peaked roof. The additional tiers

---

5. Also see research by Aryanti (2014), Kern (1956), and Lubis & Khoo (2003).

A *bedug* at rest

reflect the symbolic importance of the mosque. These tiers create a unique profile for the mosques; the lower tiers have a uniform or similar slope and the top tier is transformed into a steeply pitched turret. Stand anywhere in the Minangkabau Highlands and one faces a volcano mountaintop. Off in the distance or close up, there are great cones reaching to the sky. If one is to think about offering prayers to the heavens these majestic mountains offer a symbolic form (and reasons to pray for no eruptions).

Many of the square prayer halls imitate a cube, the height of the roof peak equalling the dimension of the square. The cube provides a large open space with no sense of hierarchy. Over time, the *mihrab* niche, and the entry became protrusions off the main square prayer hall. Often the Minangkabaus utilized these annexes to place a traditional saddle-backed roof. This saddle shape, combined with the ascending tier roofs, forms the signature elements of a traditional West Sumatran mosque. All the mosques have the ancient *bedug* (the traditional

drum) in a position of honour. Although no longer used for the daily calls to prayer, the *bedug* is still drummed for the annual Ramadan and Eid festivals. In the Minangkabau Highlands, few wash their feet before entering the mosque. In this land of water and rice, worshippers appear unconcerned about feet or what they carry into the mosque.

Most of these mosques were constructed before the arrival of the Dutch in the Minangkabau lands and even those built in the 18th or 19th century continued the traditional building style. Later mosques were no longer raised on wood posts, and solid masonry walls appeared. The Dutch colonials brought metal roofing, of which zinc-coated corrugated metal roofing became the standard, and concrete, which has replaced the traditional use of wood as the major building material. And then there are the domes, once again imported to Sumatra, which have been used to retrofit many of the old mosques. As more Sumatrans were able to make the hajj, the haji returned with the idea that a dome equalled Islam. Some scholars[6] believe that the Dutch wanted to control Islam by creating their own brand of mosque: one with a mixture of non-traditional elements, such as domes, arches and minarets. The Dutch colonialists, although often cruel and exploitative, understood the need to support indigenous culture as a means of pacification. By the 1900s, the variant mosque had arrived, outfitted with domes, minaret and remnants of the many tiered roof. This new ground-based mosque has proven especially vulnerable to the frequent earthquakes that shake the island landscape. The September 30, 2009 earthquake that devastated Padang Pariaman district caused damage to many of the area mosques, especially those with a masonry structure.[7] The wooden structures have suffered less. Over centuries, the local builders had adjusted to the periodic tremblings of the earth by inserting keyed connections between posts and bases and adding layers of horizontal bracings that connect central and auxiliary posts.

In Sumatra, a village or a group of villages built a mosque. Because of the importance of community in Sumatran culture, farmers lived not in isolated homes but congregated together in villages. Not funded by the wealthy or royalty these are true 'peoples' mosques. Gathering the timbers, carving them, framing posts, beams and rafters with no nails, and finishing the composition with handmade palm fibre roofing, the mosques are communal (cooperative) efforts, a tradition characteristic of the Sumatran people.

Padang Pariaman

Up the coast from Padang, the capital of West Sumatra, a series of wooden mosques and *surau* survive in the midst of paddy fields, coconut palms, and tropical fruit trees. Being close to the coast and to ancient ports, this region traces its religion back to several of the original founder-clerics/Sufi scholars. The volcano Mount Marapi is always out in the distance—a perfect model for the ever-ascending roofs of the mosques.

The British Library has embarked on an effort to digitize the surviving ancient Sufi manuscripts of the region. These contain texts on Islamic law, Sufism, mysticism, history and medicine. Prior to the arrival of Islam there were scant written texts in Sumatra. Jawi, or Arabic Malay, developed in the 17th century and was utilized by the Sufi scholars writing the manuscripts.

The name most often mentioned in connection with the expansion of Islam in this area is Sheikh Burhanuddin Ulakan or Shaykh Burhan al-Din (1646–1704), "Islamizer of the Minangkabau... and founder of a school at Ulakan." (Laffan 2011) Mosques in this area were either founded, built, or connected to Sheikh Burhanuddin. The Sheikh introduced mysticism in the late 17th century to Sumatra. He was born in a tiny village north of Padang. Supposedly, as a child, he and his family were adherents of Buddhism. Later, after conversations with travelling Muslims (some say merchants), the family converted. The Sheikh studied in Aceh for 10 years with the teacher Abd al-Ra'uf al-Sinkili (d. 1693), who was born near

6. Abidin Kusno writes that the Dutch brought in the dome in the late 19th century to remove 'Javanese' from Islam. (*The Appearance of Memory* 2010, 211)
7. The 1926 earthquake in nearby Padang Panjang also caused damage; notably most of the collapsed houses were made of brick. The local mosque survived while the surrounding masonry structures and minaret crumpled.

Surau Sheikh Burhanuddin. The original structure remains, with new floorboards and exterior boards placed during a recent upgrade.

Pasai (in northern Sumatra) and studied in the Gulf, Yemen, Makkah, and India. Abd al-Ra'uf al Sinkili brought the Shattariyah order to Aceh. (Laffan 2011, 18–19) After his studies, Burhanuddin returned to Ulakan and set up a mosque and *surau* inspired by the Shattariyah Sufi[8] brotherhood.

Surau Sheikh Burhanuddin sits in the sleepy village of Ulakan. Signs of the Sheikh's importance are still visible. A large boarding school offers religious instruction. The original *surau* sits in a compound with more recent buildings. A collection of mosques/*surau* presents a veritable history of mosque-building. All of the new structures, even when built with a concrete frame, maintain the typology of raised structure and many-tiered roof.

Entering the oldest structure, one is immediately struck by the forest of columns. All 16 interior posts have some form of bend, sway or lean.

Locals explain: "trees don't grow straight so the columns aren't straight". In Sumatra, there exists a long tradition of placing a building post in the direction it grew. This keeps the column and the building animate, still growing upward. The columns have been worked so that they are eight-sided[9] and some of them have repairs of new wood integrated with the old. The four central columns reach over 10 meters high to support the top (third) tier of the roof. Between some of the posts, ceiling boards have been added. The guardians say it keeps the bird droppings down. Luckily the timber framing is still visible, albeit sheathed with shiny new corrugated metal roofing.

The entire structure is raised one to one and a half metres above the ground, once again following the island tradition of raised buildings. All of the wood poles sit on a stone base. The base and the pole are connected by a wooden joint that inserts

---

8. More on the path of Sufis and Islam in West Sumatra can be found in Dobbin (1983) and Fathurahman (2003).

9. This distinctive octagonal shape, a long-standing practice in the region, can also be found in the traditional *rumah*.

into a stone opening. The roof is three-tiered. The top tier is a surprise. Instead of the usual cone, a classic Minangkabau saddle *gonjong* roof has been constructed. Somehow the builders have inserted the rectangular saddle on the square.

Surau Baru Bintungan Tinggi was built sometime in the 1700s. According to the British Library manuscript survey, this *surau* holds a great number of ancient manuscripts. The petite structure with raised floor has a single centre column that soars up to the roof peak. From the carved central column, eight horizontal beams radiate out to support eight outer columns. The vertical columns rise up to support the upper roof. Because the interior remains completely open, the forest of rafters that constitutes the roof structure is clearly visible. Clerestory-like ventilation bands separate the three tiers of roof. The *mihrab* juts out towards Makkah with a classic Minangkabau

horned roof. Originally the roofing was *ijuk* (palm fibre) but for many years it has been zinc corrugated panels.

The mosque guardian, Ramayar, is a descendent of Sheikh Bintungan Tinggi, who was a student of Sheikh Burhanuddin. Her son Tuanku Mudo Asdil is the present imam. Ramayar appears to live in the mosque. Her goods are stored in a corner. She is the watchman/caretaker in this garden of delights, surrounded by paddy fields, coconuts and peace.

The *surau* serves local rice farmers and spice growers. Young men come for lessons in the evening, and children come to learn the Qur'an. The remnants of a kitchen sit in a small adjacent building with the classic three-tiered roof and lovely vegetal-form stone carvings. It may be that this structure originally served as housing for young men.

A classic raised, all-wood structure, Surau Baru Bintungan Tinggi

Land of the Volcanoes

To travel into the Minangkabau Highlands is to discover a region blessed with rich rice fields and dominated by volcanoes, Mount Marapi being the central and most dominant. The landscape is pristine and offers few hints of the Padri wars of colonial times (1803–38). The Padris sought a purer Islam along with separation from the Dutch colonialists. They saw Sheikh Burhanuddin as a hero for his stance against the Dutch but found his Islam was too affected by local traditions. Padri leaders preached a fundamentalism that continues up to the present, disregarding local tradition in favour of an Arabian purism. For the Mandailing people just north of Minangkabau territory, the combination of Padri demands for conversion and Dutch expansion of colonialism was devastating. Assaulted from all sides, it could be said that the Mandailings were the only Southeast Asians who were forced to convert to Islam. In fact, the Padri wars and excessive Dutch laws on labour and crop cultivation forced many Sumatrans to emigrate to Malaysia, where the British had established a more open trading environment. The end result was the present large population of Sumatran Malaysians.

Typically, the old mosques are elevated at least one metre above the ground and topped by a tiered roof. The rafters have been crafted to have a slight lift at the eave. This detail is ideal for the tropical monsoon rains, slowing the descent of water. The lift/swoop at the mosque eaves is another form of homage to the Minangkabau buffalo-horn roof. Most of the mosques discussed below are from the early 19th century, but a few are from the early 1700s. The tradition of raised pole construction continued, but the details became more refined. The distinctive saddle-backed Minangkabau roof which we saw used for the *mihrab* and entry in Pariaman can be seen in the adjacent village houses and in several, but not all, of the mosques. All of the mosques are clustered around and below the majestic volcanoes.

Masjid Bingkudu sits literally at the foot of Mount Marapi. Perhaps it should be called the "Mosque of Blue". A delicious collection of shades of blue defines the exterior and interior surfaces. The

The lush Minangkabau Highlands with the ever-present volcano mountain

Prayer hall at Masjid Bingkudu; TOP Detail of column crown

village that supports the mosque sits at an altitude of 1,050 metres above sea level. The building is 19 meters from ground to peak, rising up like the neighbouring volcano. A large pond sits adjacent to the mosque. Historic photos give a sense of the strong relationship between landscape and mosque, but recent renovations have shrunk the pond. Masjid Bingkudu was founded in 1823 by Padri adherents in the midst of the Padri war.

A 2014 restoration covered the three-tiered roof with ghastly corrugated metal tiles. This was an attempt to use a material resembling clay tiles, but the metal is really just a 21st-century version of corrugated zinc roofing. A 1989 restoration led by the government had returned the palm fibre roofing, but the community couldn't wait to get rid of that organic material. They raised the entirety of funds required for the 2014 update, probably convinced that they would be freed of roof maintenance. The swoop of the roof tiers can still be seen, but obviously is much reduced by the metal tiles.

However, the 21 metre square interior hall maintains a soothing cool in contrast with the garish exterior. Sky blue wooden walls meet sky blue ceiling. The centre post is almost a metre in diameter. Surrounding it are eight posts of about 40 centimetres in diameter. The outermost series of posts are thinner and vary in diameter. Each column is topped by lovely carved red leaf bouquets and most of the columns are fluted with 12 or 16 sides. An elaborately carved *mimbar* glows in the peaceful interior. The carvings

display a 1906 date. The building has a raised floor and the wood floorboards are pristine. At the entry there is an elevated front porch with a small turret for the call to prayer. An original tower was struck by lightning and this new one was built in the 1950s.

The entire mosque is wood: floor, poles, walls, rafters. The local congregation states that everything is held together with wooden pegs, no nails. The main structure is built with "madang serai", a native Sumatra tree. The first two tiers of the roof are similar in slope and depth, but the final tier is taller and steeper. Horizontal carved boards connect the columns and continue the motifs of the *mimbar*. A series of beautiful old hanging lights adds the final touch.

Masjid Tuo Koto Nan Ampek[10] sits in the town of Payakumbuh, located in the hills below another of the volcanic mountains, Mount Sago. Built sometime between 1832 and 1840, mosque construction was led by three local princes from three different Minangkabau tribes: Datuk Kuniang from the Kampai, Datuk Pangkai Sinaro from the Pilang and Datuk Sui Dirajo, a Malay.

This mosque has been spruced up, but the structural poles and rafters, floors and walls are all the original wood. The thatch roofing rotted away and was replaced with the ever-popular zinc. The prayer hall is a square, measuring 20 metres a side. In the main building there are a number of poles which are decidedly not at 90 degrees to the floor. But the composition appears stable. The floor is

---

10. "Ampek" is Minang for the Indonesian "empat", which translates to "four". The number four is important to the Minang as a reference to the four *adat* laws for human relations. Koto Nan Ampek is the local area where the mosque sits. Masjid Tuo is how the mosque is sited, not Masjid Tua (old mosque). The mosque is also referred to as Masjid Gadang Balai Nan Ampek.

elevated about 1.2 metres from the ground. Carved and painted panels form the two clerestories. The always-present pool sits adjacent to the *mihrab*.

Neighbouring the mosque is a distinctive *rumah gadang*, the family home of one of the three princes who built the masjid. This large regal *rumah* faces the mosque entrance. Similar carvings embellish both structures. In the past, rice barns (a miniature Minang house) would sit in front of the big house. Here, one still stands, a relic of another time.

Masjid Limo Kaum has outdone its neighbours and is known for its five-tiered roof. The congregation

Roofscape at Masjid Limo Kaum

View of the multitude of columns at the prayer hall. These support five tiers of roof.

was first established (in a much simpler structure) at a different location, in the mid-17th century, at the time of Islam's entry to the Minangkabau Highlands. It is possible that this original structure was a *surau* with a three-tiered roof.[11] The mosque was built at the present location in 1710. The site is at the middle of the "Five People" (Lima Kaum) District, and close to Batusangkar, capital of the Tanah Datar Region.

As anyone who views the mosque can imagine, construction would have been a huge effort for the villagers. Historical sources stress that the mosque was assembled as a community effort. The entire structure is wood (poles, walls, beams, rafters, flooring), all collected from the nearby hills by the villagers. The original roofing was palm fibre, later replaced by zinc. Over time, the open ceiling was closed at the third tier of the roof and an attic formed.

The five tiers (*lima tingkat*) of the roof are all concave in shape. There are no gutters and all the water runs off the many tiers of roofs to a channel that runs around the mosque. This channel then empties into ponds located to the east of the entry.

A 55-metre main mast rises to the peak where a lighthouse-like crown finishes the composition. Around the main mast a spiral stair ascends to the top. The stair is sheathed, making the centre column appear even more massive. The climb to the top appears to be seldom taken. The ascent on tiny wedge treads spirals up through cobwebs, dust, broken glass, animal and bird droppings. But the view from the top is magnificent, a vista

of mountains, coconut palms and traditional roofs. If the call to prayer were to be issued from this viewpoint it would be daily inspiration for the muezzin.

Locals state that the prayer hall has 121 wooden columns, which honour the 121 elders of Lima Kaum. This forest of columns is also necessary to support the multiple tiers of roof framing. The number 121 must include some upper columns because a counting at the main floor level did not reach 121. All of the posts have been worked although the original bows and leans are still visible. The tradition of a column maintaining a tree's direction of growth has been followed. A coconut wood *bedug* remains in the prayer hall, resting on horizontal cross beams that span the outer row of posts.

An entry portico is to the east, probably added at a later date. The roofs of the entry, the *mihrab* and the prayer hall all are topped by eight-sided, enclosed, glazed lighthouses. Surely these were added at a later date, probably inspired by the style of the imported minarets that were sprouting at mosques. The exterior wood siding and glass jalousies at the windows were also added. However, the overall form of the mosque retains its integrity.

Masjid Ishlah, Masjid Tua Minangkabau Pariangan

According to a legend the first ancestor of the Minangkabau descended from Mount Marapi and settled in Pariangan village on the slopes of the mountain. The village is built between hot springs used for bathing and Nagari Pariangan, a large

---

11. Aryanti conjectures that this was a surau, 2014.

Masjid Ishlah centres the village of Pariangan, surrounded by a mix of traditional and new homes

paddy field. The hot springs originate at Mount Marapi. Local seers believe that this water can cure many diseases.

Time appears to have paused in this exquisitely sited village, the oldest settlement in the area. A river borders the village and a mix of traditional and recent houses climb up the hill. Some houses display the signature Minangkabau saddle-back roof and others are of more recent vintage. A large pool sits southwest of the prayer hall. The composition of pool, mosque and river edge creates a tiny village piazza, a gathering place for villagers. Sheikh Burhanuddin is credited with the founding of the mosque, which probably has been rebuilt many times since then.

The mosque has the typical three-tiered roof, a two-tiered *mihrab* protrusion and a portico with a lower tier roof and pyramid top similar to the prayer hall.

The top tier on mosque and portico has a steeper slope than the lower roofs. Each pyramid roof is crowned with a metal *mustaka*, a composition of globes and vertical shafts. The mosque sits on a raised stone base that also circles the exterior of the prayer hall. The prayer hall has eight-sided squat carved pillars. Four frame an elevated central area with a patterned wood band of air vents between the first and second tier of the roof. The columns all have new tiled pedestal bases. Varnished ceiling boards installed at the first roof tier form a pattern that reflects the rafter directions. Carved ventilation panels sit above each glazed window.

Masjid Tuanku Pamansiangan could be named the "Mosque of Reflection". This mosque and the just discussed Masjid Ishlah are classic Minangkabau Highlands village mosques, sharing similar structure profiles and settings. Standing at the end of a long narrow road that heads off into

Reflections of the pond onto the walls of Masjid
Tuanku Pamansiangan

city. The communal nature of villages in past times
is still visible in Kota Laweh, truly the "Land of
Ponds under the Mountain".

The masjid is well cared for. Both exterior and
interior wood present a rich patina from a white
well-worn paint. Reflections from the ponds which
surround the mosque dapple the wooden walls.
In this land of ponds, every home seems to be
surrounded by pools, which are used to raise fish.
The pools merge into the rice field ponds through
numerous channels and rivulets.

Inside the prayer hall a large centre column rises up.
The attendant says that it goes from base-ground
(sitting on a large flat rock) to top of roof (almost
nine metres). What a feat it must have been to place
this giant central pole which centres the mosque
and the community. The mosque has a total of nine
poles and they were all said to be brought down
from Mount Marapi. All of the columns are topped
by a variant of the carved red leaf bouquets found
at Masjid Bingkudu. There is an elegant and simple
mimbar. A story is inscribed on this wooden pulpit,
but no one in this community can read Arabic, so
the story is a story that is mentioned but not told.
The traditional drum holds its place of honour at
the corner of the prayer room.

According to local sources, the mosque was
founded and built by Tuanku Pamansiangan, a
student of Sheikh Burhanuddin. However, the
mosque was built in 1825 and the Sheikh died in
1704, so Tuanku was probably taught by a student
of a student of the Sheikh. Tuanku moved to
this village—Kota Laweh—and built the mosque
sometime during the Padri War. He served as
imam and his grave is just up the hill from
the mosque.

the jungle, the mosque literally sits in the shadow
of Mount Marapi. The village is composed of
fine old homes, with hardly any of the clutter of
advertisements, car repair shops and noise of the

A celebration of carving traditions is found on the outside walls of Masjid Asasi Nagari Gunung. This mosque is very much like a traditional Minangkabau house in the quantity of wall carvings.

Masjid Asasi Nagari Gunung[12]

Called the "Human" (*asasi* translates as original or first) mosque, this mosque was established in 1770, or in 1685 (according to Dutch chroniclers). Listed as the oldest mosque in Padang Panjang, it was built by four tribal communities. The mosque displays an original centre pole that is a metre or more in diameter and approximately 15 metres high. The original *ijuk* roof was replaced in 1912— palm to zinc. The *mihrab* protrusion has the typical buffalo-horn shape roof. The *bedug* has its own mini-Minang house out in front of the masjid.

The exterior is completely covered in carvings, which residents say were redone in a 2011 renovation. The only original carvings are on the two upper clerestories. This mosque is very much like a traditional Minangkabau house in the quantity of wall carvings.

The symbolism of the carving motifs has been mainly forgotten over the years, but according to interviews with master carvers "what was essential was the ability to continue to re-create the forms". (Capistrano, 31) A consistent use of natural forms reflects a local belief that one looks to nature for guidance in life. There is a similarity of pattern between these wood carvings and the textile weaving patterns of the traditional *songket* cloth. Textiles were an important part of *adat*, which guided birth, marriage, death and more. By using these patterns, the carvers would be relying on well-established forms. In the past, the preferred colours were green, a deep red,

12. Gunung is the Indonesian word for mountain. Many of the mosques have the word inserted in their official titles.

black and purple. Patterns of fern leaf tendrils and baby ducks in motion signify an emphasis on cooperation. Four- and eight-pointed stars are another common motif.[13] A border surround symbolizes the village which is bound by *adat*. The original carvings on the clerestory display the traditional border and four-pointed stars, along with a profusion of leaf forms.

After this display of carvings, another surprise awaits in the interior. All the ceilings are swooped, rounded, and finished in varnished wood planks. Bent wooden boards give the feeling of being inside a sailing boat, snug and safe, probably a reference to the ancient traditions and stories about the Minangkabau connections to the sea and ships. The grand centre column steps back in three gradations as it ascends. The outer posts display the typical multisided woodworking while the bases appear to be sheathed in a multitude of wood strips.

On the grounds of the mosque, an old warehouse is said to hold a cache of old manuscripts. Besides ancient writings, the mosque has one more special feature: a spring that has been a continuous source of water for centuries. Used for ablutions, the water also serves neighbourhood parents who bring their children to the spring house for bathing.

Surau Nagari Lubuk Bauk. Local lore has it that the structure was a joint effort of four local tribes, reflected in the unique four-sided crown roof. The *surau* was built between 1884 and 1896 and restored in 1984. Some attribute an earlier date of 1809. Outside, the traditional drum can

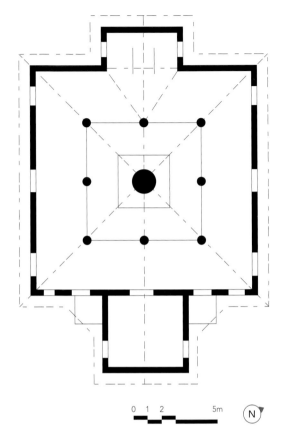

Plan of Masjid Asasi Nagari Gunung

be found in its own miniature Minang house, all bordered by the ever-present ponds. The structure was probably used for a time as the community mosque. Today, it has returned to its original use as school and community meeting place. Adjacent to the venerable *surau*, a new concrete "box" with a "flying saucer" on top has been built to serve as the mosque.

The *surau* is entered on sweeping concrete stairs, typical of many Malay/Sumatran homes. All else is timber and the walls reveal the same plank

---

13. Gayle, 1989. Her thesis examines textile patterns in Sumatra.

system as a traditional house. The beamed ceiling at the peak of the first roof tier has wood plank floorboards, which provide a second storey for study rooms. Whereas the space between the two tiers of roof is usually composed of ventilation boards, this second floor perimeter has a full height opening with a balcony railing wrapping the perimeter. A ladder allows ascent up into the lighthouse crown where there is a spectacular view of a series of pools and the surrounding countryside. Both the *mihrab*

annex and the top roof tier have a unique four-sided saddle roof. At the peak sits a glazed lighthouse crown, which is crowned with a *mustaka* composed of a series of globes. Lighthouse crowns appear in many of the mosques of the 18th century. Eventually they became exterior structures that functioned as minarets.

This *surau* and the preceding Masjid Asasi have several similarities. Both are located in or near

The prayer hall at Masjid Asasi Nagari Gunung has an interior that speaks to wooden ships

Exterior of Surau Nagari Lubuk Bauk, with a plethora of carved panels and a fantasy roofscape

Detail of painted carving

View of the surrounding ponds from the rooftop

the town of Padang Panjang, both were built by four tribes and both have a wealth of carving with similar colourings. The gable surfaces created in the roof saddle ends are filled with carvings, rafter ends at the eaves display the ubiquitous leaf ends, the *mirhab* exterior has traditional carvings of flower and leaf with a horizontal border at top and bottom, and the drum house has carvings on all four exterior surfaces. The structures are raised and at the floor level, simple but elegant carved bands mark the perimeter.

Solok

Travelling south, the landscape changes. Tea plantations dominate, not the rich rice paddies found further north. Another volcano, Gunung Talang, stands guard over the villages. The people seem poorer, living in a high valley with steep sided flanks. In the past, a Sumatran without rice paddy had a less secure existence for he lacked the reliable asset of family rice to feed the family.

Masjid Tuo Kayu Jao sits in a valley of green. The mosque displays the signature form of early Sumatran mosques and continues to be maintained by villagers who renew the traditional palm fiber roofing.

Masjid Tuo Kayu Jao. This small and humble mosque has a raised timber construction approximately 10 metres square, with a simple set of stairs at the entry door and no portico. The *mihrab* juts outward and is roofed with a classic Minangkabau *gonjong* roof. At this mosque can be seen a palm fibre roof, renewed often by the villagers. Built in 1599, it is one of the oldest extant mosques in Sumatra.

One timber column has been replaced but the remaining twenty-six are original. Twenty-seven pillars stand as four columns for each of the six tribes and three for the main personages of a mosque: the *khatib* (preacher), the imam, and the *bilal* (caller to prayer). All of the columns have been shaped into multisided pillars. The mosque has 13 windows, a reference to the 13 principles of prayers in Islam.

The last restoration involved painting the structure a dark brown, which darkens the feel of this little jewel, sitting at the bottom, and the end, of a tiny village road. The three-tiered roof with concave slopes is crowned with a pyramid, albeit a more humble pyramid then some of the bigger mosques. Topping the pyramid is a metal *mustaka*. Carved air vents set between each roof tier consist of round *mandala*s set between vertical patterned boards. Some of the vent-carving details are repeated at the pulpit inside, considered by many to be the original. The fibre roof is finished with decorative punched metal bindings at the ridges. At the hips, the fibre is gathered into a long roll, bound with metal pieces and placed at the junction between roof planes. The fibre roofing and detailing fully display the graceful curves of the roof structure. This vision is unfortunately missing at many of the old mosques as they have been sheathed in hard materials that conceal the lovely swoops.

A long *bedug* is housed in its own rectangular open structure facing the entry. This drum is claimed to be the original. Running alongside the drum house and south of the prayer hall, a stream (Batang Marus) races down the steep hill. Another designation for this magical compound would be "Mosque of the Sound of Running Water". The sound of the stream is startlingly strong in the peaceful valley. Besides the isolation and lack of cars, no intrusive loudspeakers are used for the call to pray.

There is a wealth of historic fabric in West Sumatra. The question is how to maintain this resource and protect it from plastic roofing, incompatible additions, lowered ceilings, domes and minarets, and even demolition. At most mosques the manager collects money and then it is he who decides what should happen. These managers are uneducated in conservation, so they put in false ceilings, place tiles on old wooden surfaces, paint with non-traditional colours. Conservationists believe that the mosque interior roof structures were once all exposed. Interior changes wrought by mosque administrators reduce the airflow in the building and alter the visual power of the roof tiers. Buildings are often re-roofed with metal panels, composite tiles or other new intrusive materials. These roofing materials reduce the emblematic shape of the Minangkabau roof, although it must be said that the old zinc roofing adheres more to

the shape than the newer products. It would be hoped that a more subtle and responsive roofing material could be developed for the historic roofs of both mosques and houses.

Looking at old photos, there is a repeating motif of mosque surrounded by large ponds. Today, at many sites, the remains of a pond (walls and recessed areas) can be seen, but the ample bodies of water that formed part of the mosque composition have been reduced or removed. Will the mosque grounds one day consist only of a path around the structure? There should be concern for the setting as well as the building: the form in relation to its context. The integrity of the entire composition needs recognition.

The challenge is how to celebrate the wooden construction and encourage the continued use of the mosque, keeping the mosque alive and functioning. Speaking of Sumatran and Minangkabau culture, Susan Rodgers writes "…history often has a physical, tactile form in Southeast Asia." (1995, 27) Sumatrans have a strong connection to the objects of their past. That desire to maintain these physical contacts with the past can assist in the ongoing efforts to maintain the historic mosques, an important part of every Sumatran's sense of being. The *masjid tua* is not a museum but a place of prayer. It should remain a living dynamic structure. These mosques are the creations of ancestors who invested energy and passion into creating a uniquely Sumatran community mosque.

Java
Pavilions for Prayer

———⌒———

"Now at that time in Java's land
All had become Moslem
There was none who did resist
All the mountain hermits
The ascetics and acolytes
the devotees and disciples
Many converted to the faith

...

The desire of all the wali
The eight who made the relic
A little something rather grand
Was to create a new mosque
A sacred site of power for the kingdom of Demak
A pusaka *for all the kings*
Of all the Land of Java"

Florida 1995, 320–21

Java is the land of princes, kingdoms and volcanoes. The site of ancient civilizations, for centuries the island has been the centre of high culture in the Indonesian archipelago. Positioned on the southern edge of the Straits of Malacca, Javanese ports were the next stop after Sumatra and served as connectors to the much sought-after products of the Spice Islands (the Maluku Islands or the Moluccas). Just as pepper brought traders to the Malabar Coast from faraway Europe, the cloves and nutmeg of the Moluccas seduced merchants from China to the Mediterranean. Along Java's lengthy northern coast, cities grew in response to the need to hold and transport merchandise, especially cloth and spices.

Documents marking the land of Java can be found in ancient Indian and Chinese texts. Even the Romans knew of Java, Ptolemy appears to refer to Java in Roman Empire maps. And just as the religions of India (Hinduism and Buddhism) arrived on the Javanese shores with traders, so too did the faith of Islam. Starting in the 15th century, the presence of Muslims is noted in travel journals. By the 17th century Islam was becoming the dominant religion of the island. Indonesia,

Pilgrims at Masjid Agung Demak immediately head to the four central wood columns.

the sprawling archipelago nation, has the largest Muslim population in the world. The island of Java is home to the majority of the country's Indonesians and Muslims, the densest and most populated island in the world.[1] Java is also home to three distinct language/cultural groups: the Javanese, Sundanese and Madurese. In this chapter we will be mainly examining the Javanese.

Islam arrived by ship at the north coast seaports, the *pasisir*, and then spread inland. The *pasisir* was the holding area for spices coming from the Moluccas and for goods from throughout Asia.

Commodities were shipped to China, India, the Middle East and on to the Mediterranean. In 1515, Pires wrote in his *Suma Oriental*:

> "Some of them [the merchants] were Chinese, some Arabs, Parsees, Gujuraties, Bengalees and of many other nationalities and they flourished so greatly that Mohammad and his followers are determined to introduce their doctrine in the sea coast of Java [together] with merchandise".

Only one part of Indonesia, a nation of over ten thousand islands, Java is nonetheless the economic

---

1. In 2014 the population of Java was around 140 million, with a density of over 1,130 people/square kilometer.

centre and capital. Long before the Europeans arrived, an extensive maritime network connected the Middle East to India and from there to the archipelago and China. The two islands of Java and Sumatra were the major trading points for world trade.

> "...for centuries before the Europeans arrived, Arab and Asian traders did business in the independent fiefdoms of the archipelago, without feeling the need to bind them into a whole. They were helped along by the winds, which have driven long-distance trade for most of human history. Around the equator, the winds change direction mid-year. That provided a convenient conveyor belt between China and India, the two powerhouses of production and consumption at the time. ...Anyone who wanted to ship silk and muslin, ceramics and metalwork, tea and silver between India and China had either to climb the Himalayas or to pass through what are now Indonesian waters."(Pisani 2014, 10-11)

Formed by volcanoes, Java benefits from extraordinarily rich soil. The sumptuous agricultural land and high rice yields produced a population density that could support an extensive royal court. There was enough wealth to sustain royal centres where scholars and artisans could thrive. Java, more than any other island in the archipelago, nurtured kingdoms that left behind monumental structures. In Java, Islam encountered "one of Asia's greatest political, aesthetic, religious and social creations, the Hindu-Buddhist Javanese state." (Geertz 1968, 11)

The 15th century brought the realization to the Javanese that they were not the centre of the universe. The expansion of trade and the arrival of Islam made them aware of their limits and of the need to set new boundaries. The Javanese needed to integrate their cultural identity with the new religion of Islam in order to maintain their world view. "Islam, like Java, is both local and global at the same time." (Kusno 2010, 207& 215)

Populated by natives and the descendants of a diaspora of travellers/settlers (Chinese, Yemenites, Gujaratis, Malays, Tamils, Malabari, Batak, Dutch, British, Bugis, Acehnese, and on and on), Java can best be described as syncretic. Taking a little from here, a bit from there, a culture grew, religions ripened, people created identities. The anthropologist Clifford Geertz believed that societies, including the Indonesians, create "a structure of difference within which cultural tensions that are not about to go away, or even to moderate, can be placed and negotiated—contained in a country".(Geertz 2000, 257) Abidin Kusno described it thus: "...Java, through incessant attempts to accommodate, adapt, and resist historical phenomena, transforms itself even as it acknowledges the difficulty of the transformation, the expression of which, quite often, is the essence of Java itself." (Kusno 2010, 206)

It is the syncretic nature of Java, a land of difference, which guided the creation of the early mosques. Mosques replaced the temples and shrines of the earlier gods. But the Javanese people were not ready to completely discard their ancient practices. These traditions, called *adat*, as in Sumatra, remained deep in the hearts of the people. The strength of the new religion was its ability to take contrasting strands and merge them into one new belief, a belief that Geertz calls "multivoiced". Scholars have all noted that the Muslims arrived with trade. They did not come as conquerors, as did the Portuguese and the

Spanish, nor did they impose themselves or their religion on the native inhabitants as occurred in North India. The mosques symbolized a gathering of all things Javanese into a new structure for Islam. Josef Prijomoto wrote:

> "local traditions were taken over without difficulty; and the Muslims even used the existing forms of buildings, apart from a few changes necessitated by the new ritual ... This evidence shows that the coming of Islamic culture did not loosen the strong bond of the Javanese culture with the past." (Prijomoto 1984, 23–24)

The mosque builders turned not to the monumental Hindu/Buddhist stone shrines built to hold and honour only the gods, but to the pavilion, the *pendopo* (or *pendapa*), a ubiquitous form in Java dedicated to community gatherings. Since a mosque must accommodate in one grand space the community for prayer, the expansive pavilions better fit the purpose of a religious structure, both for a prayer hall and for the surrounding veranda. An open, airy, proportioned, post and beam structure with pitched, rain shedding roofs serves as gathering space, public space, and religious space. For the mosque, the builders added a multi-tiered roof. There is an abundance of theories on the reasons for such a multi-tiered roof. Certainly, as in Sumatra, the cone shapes of mountains and volcanoes form important symbols in Javanese culture. In the ancient stone *candi*,[2] the vertical dominates, often stepping up to a cone shaped top. The single ending point of the peaked roof is the ultimate connector to the cosmos. There is a long tradition of multiple tiered roofs, many still visible in the pagodas of Bali. Some relate the tiers to Islamic teachings, and Tajudeen believes that the three-tiered roof may be a reference to the three cosmic realms (the underworld, the middle world of humans and the upper world of good spirits) that were an important part of the Javanese spiritual world.[3] As another scholar writes: "Java is exceptional in the Islamic world not because it has retained pre-Islamic ideas but because of the ingenious and artful ways in which such a large body of Hindu and Buddhist traditions have been thoroughly Islamicized." (Woodward 1989, 17) The majority agree that the ancient mosque style is genuinely Indonesian, adapted from the building traditions of the previous era.[4]

Pavilions have a series of columns that support a sloping timber-framed roof. The wooden columns sit on a stone base. Cut down, the great trees sit on a base that represents the tree's former roots, the leafy top is now the column crown. To solve the problem of buckling at the tall interior columns of the mosque, the builders thickened the centre pillars and added circular iron bands and horizontal bracing.

Without walls the breezes, sounds, and smells of the city drift through the open pavilion space. All the ancient palace compounds contained a series of pavilions—each serving a different purpose. Royal pavilions were used for meetings, for formal occasions and ceremonies, for *gamelan* concerts,

---

2. A structure of stone or brick that serves as a shrine or temple to a deity, typically Hindu or Buddhist. These pyramidal towers are found throughout Indonesia and reflect the symbolic strength of the mountain.
3. *Architecturalized Asia* 2013, 135.
4. Jacques Dumarcay has closely examined the construction techniques of Java and Southeast Asia. A series of articles and books excellently illustrate the timber structure.

The large veranda graces the east side of Masjid Agung Mataram in Kotagede, the first royal seat of the Mataram Empire.

A typical Javanese pavilion; this one is used for the neighbourhood *gamelan*.

Exterior view of the grand veranda and many roofed royal mosque in Surakarta. Note the *mustaka* or rooftop crown, versions of which can be seen on most historic Javanese mosques.

their volcanic earth. Houses, markets, palaces, temples and mosques rise up from this base. Javanese development, unlike Sumatran, instigated urban spaces; the city builders demanded sturdy ground-based structures.

Pavilions can be huge, with an army of columns supporting multiple layers of roofs. Stone carvings of open pavilions can be found on the illustrated storyline that forms the lower levels of the stunning Borabadur, the ninth-century Javanese sacred site. "...in Java's Hindu and Buddhist sanctuaries since the eighth century and in its Islamic palaces and mosques since the 15th century one finds hip-roof pavilions on plinths..."[6]

The mosques are big, square, high-roofed, timber-framed buildings. The prayer hall roofs ascend upward in a series of sloped planes, crowned by a pyramidal tier. One knows it is a mosque not because there is a minaret (few old Indonesian mosques have one) but because of the regal roof. Although the mosque has walls, the structure follows the *pendopo* typology of posts, beams and rafters supporting a roof. The central pillars, soaring from floor to upper roof, serve as a symbolic link between the people and their spiritual source. Typically, an open pavilion–veranda surrounds the main prayer hall, a transition from outside to inside. The grandest, the *serambi*,[7] always extends from the eastern, entry facade. For the veranda a one-tier or lower tiered

and for presentations to the common man. On a smaller scale, the *pendopo* could be found at many Javanese residences. Traditional Javanese homes presented an open pavilion toward the street or road. Here was the place to greet visitors and to entertain guests.

In much of the Malay Archipelago, buildings are built on stilts. In a land of rising and receding water it is good and important to be above the ground. Early Javanese structures conformed to this idea, but eventually Java became an exception.[5] Javanese build a solid stone base on

5. The stone base/floor can also be found in traditional buildings in Lombok and Timor.

6. Tajudeen writes of the enigmatic nature of Javanese architecture. Over centuries, the Hindu-Buddhist-Islamic constructions have often been mislabeled and misunderstood. Some want to source them to China or India whereas Tajudeen (along with Miksic, Tjahjono and O'Neil) believes that both the stone and wooden constructions are uniquely Javanese. *Architecturalized Asia* 2013, 121.

7. *Serambi* and *pendopo* are both terms used to describe the grand open pavilions/verandas of Java. The *pendopo* is often a free-standing pavilion, a *serambi* is a veranda attached to a building.

The large courtyard at the royal mosque in Yogyakarta provides much-needed space for play.

Over the years, these verandas have increased in area as the population and the need for more prayer space grew. Simple verandas expanded into huge, open, roofed platforms. In many of the old Javanese mosques this space is used by men, women and children for resting, gathering, and meeting friends. For sure, at Friday prayer the front veranda, along with the prayer hall, is ceded to prayer. But for the rest of the week, people eat, talk, and sleep; young couples meet and giggle. In a hot climate like Java's, one does not want to sit and talk under the sun, so the veranda–pavilion is a perfect stopping place.

roof is sufficient as a sign that the prayer hall is the most important. Completing the composition, a low wall encircles the compound.

When were the mosques built? One can keep asking, but a fixed date is not an Indonesian response. It is the process, the settlement, the site, and the history that is noted. Changes have been made over time. The important fact is that there was a beginning and from that point a mosque existed.

Indonesia is a 'developing' nation. Urban areas are growing at a rapid pace, infrastructure is stressed. Roads are clogged, buses packed, electricity limited, water questionable. The gracious old pavilions that used to dot residential areas are quickly disappearing. Indonesians are an outgoing, community-minded people who like to sit and talk and watch the world. The mosque verandas, the anteroom to the official praying room, have become the public gathering spaces.

Unlike the Malabar Coast and Sumatra where mosques were built by local communities, most of the Javanese mosques explored in this book were constructed by leaders as royal mosques. Built as a part of the royal compound or built at the site of royal burials or built for retainers of royalty, these mosques share a typology and a common vernacular. Of course, there were many royal families, with branches and progeny spread everywhere. "…architecture refers to not merely a reflection of the culture of a society but also the unsettling negotiations of culture and identity." (Kusno 2010, 206) For Kusno, mosque-building in Java is a political act. From Sukarno's giant independence mosque in Jakarta stretching back to the Demak and Mataram sultans, the mosque form can be seen as an invention of the culture.

Besides being a site of prayer, the old mosques of Java articulate a unique urban space. In a low-walled compound at the centre of a historic town, they sit adjacent to, but removed from, the bustling markets and crowded streets, the constant buying, selling and bargaining of daily life. The centre of the compound is, of course, the prayer hall, shimmering with an inner peace, quiet and cool. Open outside areas serve as children's play area and no one discourages a multitude of uses. All mosques provide public toilets and wash areas. But it is the open pavilions (most frequently adjacent to the prayer hall) that are the most amazing gift to the community.

Pasisir—The Coast: Cirebon, Kudus and Demak, Jepara

"The notion of the Pasisir goes beyond the geographical definition of the northern coastline of Java. This term is commonly used to define the cultures and historical experiences of people living in the micro segment of the Southeast Asian maritime world. It also extends across a trading circuit that begins from the towns on the north coast of Java and involves their corresponding trading partners. These are found on the Coromandel coasts of India, in southern China, southern Sumatra, Singapore, the Malay peninsula, Penang, southern Thailand, southern Burma, Kalimantan, as well as the islands of the eastern reach of the archipelago."
Lee 1997, 23

"Trade is the soul of a society, ...No matter how arid and empty a land might be – like Arabia, for example – if its trade flourishes so will its people prosper. Even if your country is blessed with rich and fertile land, if its trade is dead and deflated so too will everything be and so its people will remain poor. Small countries have become great because of their trade, and great countries have fallen because their trading life has withered."
Toer 1990, 263

Cirebon is a key port city on the *Pasisir* (sometimes referred to as Pesisir), the northern coast of Java. The city still maintains a bit of the look of a 16th-century Islamic city. There are palaces (quite a few since royal squabbles resulted in many divisions), a pleasure garden, a masjid *agung*, and a burial complex. Many of the traditional mosques still stand. The city is the abode of the Sultan of Cirebon and on a hill above the city is the final resting place of the Sultan's progenitor Sunan Gunung Jati. The Masjid Agung, literally the great mosque, and the Sultan's palace are located around the *alun-alun* (city's town square); the mosque on the western side, the palace on the south. A large central market sits to the north. These four elements form the heart of this "city of the palace". The ensemble endures as one of the oldest Islamic settlement structures in Java; the layout is replicated in all the royal centres.

"Cirebon .... possibly apart from Gresik in East and Kota Gede in Central Java no other Javanese city conveys such a good picture of a Javanese town from the 16/17 century – the period of transition." (Brakel & Massarik 1982)

Cirebon is strongly connected to Sunan Gunung Jati. During his reign, Cirebon became a political force and claimed an economic importance on the island of Java. Gunung Jati moved to Cirebon in 1550 and ruled until his death in 1568. Around 1628, the city became part of the Mataram Empire, and served as an important harbour for the largest and most extensive Muslim empire on Java. Eventually, the Sultanate of Cirebon was divided in two: Kanoman and Kasepuhan. Further divisions created two additional *kraton*s (palaces), Kaceribonan and Kaprabonan. The palaces and mosques of these can still be found in Cirebon today.

At this point we should pause and discuss the *wali songo* (nine saints), one of whom is Sunan

Gunung Jati. These men who brought Islam to Java are legendary on the island. Their stories fill volumes. They represent several generations of Sufi holy men known for carrying the message of Islam throughout Java. Many were born on the island, others had progenitors from all parts of the Islamic world (China to Arabia). As we investigate different mosques around the island we will meet other *wali* and learn more about their history.

Masjid Agung Kasepuhan
(Great Mosque of Cirebon)

In 2013, Imam Latief Rowatib had served the mosque for 40 years. Although he no longer leads Friday prayers, he is a source of many legends concerning the mosque. The Imam dates the mosque to 1401, although historians put the date as 1498 at the earliest. Legend has it that the construction was directed by Sunan Gunung Jati with the assistance of two other *wali songo*: Sunan Bonang and Sunan Kalijaga.[8]

This mosque, unlike Demak, which we will soon discuss, was placed at an angle to the *alun-alun* (which is positioned on the royal north–south axis) so that the orientation to Makkah is relatively accurate. Unique among the Javanese mosques discussed, this one has a rectangular plan, with the longer side being the *qibla* wall. A massive red brick wall (fifty centimetres deep) surrounds the main hall. The brick wall, with decorative vents cut into the brick, is two metres high. Not reaching the ceiling or supporting the great roof, the wall serves as a guardian and protective barrier for the prayer hall. Continuing this idea of marking space, a low brick wall surrounds the entire mosque compound.

There are nine doors (for the nine *wali*) piercing the wall. The doors openings are low in height, requiring one to bow to enter into the main prayer hall. The main entrance to the prayer hall has a two-leaf door aligned with the *qibla* axis. The door jambs are extended outwards to form massive pillars with fine carvings. Stone, rather than masonry, is used for the pillars which further accentuates their importance. The surrounding southeast brick wall is adorned with stone reliefs.

Entering the prayer hall, one is struck first by a veritable forest of columns. Thirty original round teak columns, of which twelve support the high roof, rise up to the many-tiered pyramidal roof. The mosque has a spectacular structure, the impact somewhat lessened by the 20th-century addition of steel pipe cages embracing every wooden column, a reminder of the ever-present possibility of earthquake. The roof is pyramidal, but the structure has a rectangular plan; thus, there is a short ridge and no crown.

The *mihrab* repeats the stone construction and patterns from the main entry door, including the endless knot motif. The arched niche is guarded by two cylindrical columns that are flanked by two outer flat rectangular ones. The niche recess is deep enough for the imam to stand comfortably inside it. A three-dimensional carved lotus (according to local traditions made by Sunan Kalijaga) hangs down from the ceiling of the niche.

The main hall is surrounded by expansive open pavilions added at later dates. There is a feel of ease here, people of all ages are sleeping, lounging, reading, or playing. The mosque guardian is

8. Hugh O'Neill, (in *The Mosque,* edited by Frishman 1994, 234*)* places the mosque foundation at 1500.

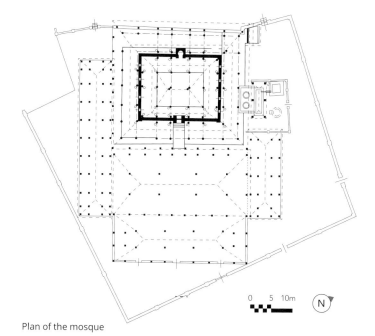

Plan of the mosque

One of the stone reliefs set in the brick wall.

Expansive verandas complete three sides of the Great Mosque (Masjid Agung Kasepuhan), Cirebon. The prayer hall brick wall can be seen on the left.

friendly, smoking cigarettes, tending cats, lounging on the vast floor, laughing heartily when asked questions about history. He may have few answers, but he exudes welcome.

Masjid Panjunan sits surrounded by a red brick wall, in a quiet neighbourhood. Little land has been left to this mosque and it is not clear if at one time it had a more spacious compound. The founder's tomb is adjacent to the prayer hall. The founder, Pangeran Panjunan, was probably related to Sunan Gunung Jati and a bit of a rebel for he built his own mosque outside the official palace mosques.[9] Some theorize that he was an Arab leader of Baghdad immigrants, others say he was a student of Sunan Gunung Jati. The mosque is sited in the old Arab quarter and was probably built in the 1550s, during the lifetime of Panjunan and the reign of Sunan Gunung Jati.

Like Masjid Agung Kasepuhan, the brick walls encircling the prayer hall do not reach the ceiling. The red bricks are all locally made. Even today Cirebon is surrounded by kilns. Brick walls in the city are left bare; no plaster is applied except at ornamental entryways. The mosque has a nine-metre square hall. The signature entry archway with sculpted plaster shapes is similar to those at the palace and at the Masjid Agung. The arch, in the Hindu-Javanese fashion, is flanked by the ever present *garuda*[10] wings. The wood superstructure is put together with no nails, the dark wood offering a rich contrast with the brick. The mosque has a modest two-tiered roof, crowned by the royal *mustaka*, an element we will see repeated in mosques throughout Java.

Carved wooden entry door at Masjid Panjunan, framed by the traditional *garuda* wings and a display of Chinese ceramics

Similar to many older structures in Cirebon, the brick walls have scores of inset Chinese plates. Most of the ceramics on the inner mosque walls are new, but some of the original plates are still embedded in the outer compound walls. The use of ceramics and tiles in Javanese mosques may have been inspired by the use of tiles in central Asia and China.

Trusmi is a village in the Cirebon city district known for batik. Since the days of the Kingdom of Cirebon the villagers have been known for their skill and creativity in sculpture (wood carving)

9. Brakel & Massarik 1982.

10. The ancient *garuda*, a character in Hindu mythology, was a bird or man-bird with great protecting wings.

The leaders of the Masjid and Makam Buyut Trusmi in one of the many pavilions in the compound

Local woman dressed in the batiks created in Trusmi

and batik. Today the area is literally awash in batik and the majority of the population is employed in the batik industry. Dyed cloth hangs on lines, ladies bend over small fires[11] and the finished cloth dazzles the eye.

The mosque at Trusmi sits inside a large complex, with a medley of buildings (for prayer, relaxing, teaching and bathing) and roofs (wood, tile shingles, and palm thatch). A large cemetery sits to one side, along with an ancient well and pool. The mosque has the classic three-tiered roof but many of the surrounding structures are capped with another classic, the pavilion *joglo*[12] roof. A brick wall with arches and two entry gates encloses the area, all fine examples of the classical art of pre-Islamic times. A quartet of male elders, with matching white diagonal cloth across their chests,

greets visitors. The *kyai* (spiritual leader) invites guests into his pavilion—an open-air low-roofed space that is rich with carvings and woven mats.

The community has a long tradition of coming together to maintain the mosque compound buildings. There is an annual celebration where the thatch roofing is renewed with new woven grasses. The teak shingles are replaced every four to eight years.

The founder of the mosque is said to have been related in some manner to Sunan Gunung Jati. Local folklore places this mosque complex as originally a 13th-century Hindu hermitage. Here, the continuity between early Javanese religious buildings and the subsequent mosque structures is readily visible.

---

11. Batik requires that a wax-resist is applied to cloth. The wax is melted in small pots over fires.

12. The *joglo* roof is the most complex and is used for the houses of royalty or the wealthy. A low-slope outer roof rises up to a steeply pitched centre roof that sits on four main columns (the *soko guru* as found in the mosque).

View of some of the many roofs at the mosque compound in Trusmi

Demak was considered the Makkah of Indonesia, the first city of the first Islamic kingdom in Java. The Demak Sultanate and the power of Java's coastal cities rose as Majahapit rule declined. The city is northeast of Semarang and was originally a seaport but now sits inland from the coast because what once was a swampy shoreline has completely silted up. The historian Andre Wink talks about the changes in river courses throughout Asia, resulting in "lost cities" and "lost rivers". (Wink 2002)

Daily, groups of pilgrims from around the nation arrive at Masjid Agung Demak and patiently wait in the open outer veranda for the prayer hall doors to open. The rest of the complex is open to the public twenty-four hours a day. There are no outside gates or guards and visitors gather freely in and around the large verandas. Our guide happily unlocked the prayer hall doors so that we could enter before the official opening time. The interior

of this very famous mosque is clean and simple with four giant round wooden columns, along with a series of brick/plaster columns. Everything is over-scaled. The massive central wooden columns are named for four of the great *wali songo*: Kalijaga, Ampel, Bonang and Gunung Jati.

According to legend, the settlement at Demak was founded in the second half of the 15th century. A granddaughter of the founder married a Muslim from North Sumatra, Sunan Gunung Jati.

The mosque is a twenty-five metre square with a three-tiered roof and a large veranda on the east. There are porticos on the northern, western, and southern sides. The four centre columns of the prayer hall, the *soko guru* (or *saka guru*), are the main supports for the upper/highest roof. In the *Babad Tanah Jawi*[13] it is written that the four pillars of the mosque were each made by one of

---

13. "History of the land of Java", a series of manuscripts in Javanese that speak of the arrival and spread of Islam in Java.

Exterior of Masjid Agung Demak; the surrounding veranda was added over the years to this mosque with a three-tiered roof.

the four guardians: southeast by Raden Rahmat (Sunan Ampel), southwest by Sunan Gunung Jati, the northwest by Sunan Bonang, and northeast by Sunan Kalijaga.

The master pillar is a mythic miracle, made from teak wood chips and fibres, which were then tied together by rope. During all the past restorations any suggestions to replace it have been rejected. To replace the master pillar would mean to annihilate the 'pusaka-ship': "The most sacred support, the ground, as it were of the monument (the realm, authority) is a marvelous composite

of residues."[14] Sunan Kalijaga was the creator of this master pillar. He gathered fragments from the work of the other *wali* and "wills the fragments one." Sunan Kalijaga is a potent symbol for Java, remembered for his humanity. He was a boy gone wrong, a bandit who then met Sunan Bonang and changed his life. He became a devout Muslim and the maker of the wood-chip pillar. (Florida 1995, 328–9) His mosque/tomb (dated 1533) sits nearby.

Stories abound about the *soko guru*. The mosque guide states that during one of the recent renovations structural supports (probably steel)

14. *Pusaka* is "a relic or trace, a monument that would stand perpetually as a concrete material site both for pilgrimage and of supernatural power." It stands as basis for Moslem kingship in Java. (Florida, 321)

were placed inside the wooden columns. Parts of the original pillars are kept in the adjacent museum. To the bare eye, the round columns seem to be composed of thick vertical wood planks with metal bands at regular intervals. The four main columns soar to over 16 metres tall. The full height of the mosque is 22 metres. As mosques often have a cubic form with height equalling the base, the addition of the roof crown might reach close to the 25 metres of the floor base.

Unfortunately, the most recent 'renovation' covered the walls and floors with tile and marble. According to archival records the original simple timber mosque was an open structure and it was only in the 19th century that a brick wall was built to surround the main hall. Several sources note that a ceiling was inserted in the mosque in 1848. If today it could be removed "the essential integrity of its impressive interior would be restored." (O'Neil in *The Mosque*, 233)

The *maqsura*, a small wooden pavilion for the king, was added sometime in the 19th century. It is located to the left of the *mihrab*. An elaborate *mimbar* is to the right, now encased in a glass box. On the *qibla* wall, there are 15th-century Vietnamese ceramics. The blue and white tiles depict flowers, foliage and some birds.

The main prayer hall doors are richly carved. Otherwise, the mosque interior displays a calming simplicity, an austere grandeur. One of the original double doors was carved with a dragon-headed beast, another element from the time of the Majapahit. The Masjid Agung Demak was built at a time of transition and the builders were reflecting on their past as they moved to the future.

At 10 a.m. the prayer hall doors open wide and masses crowd in. Men circle the columns, embracing them. Women touch the columns, lean on them and embrace them in groups. Many of the pilgrims appear to be country people. Most women wear traditional Javanese sarongs, tops and colourful head scarves. The mosque is a national monument to the *wali*. Although there have been many changes, "in all cases the façades were always determined by the dominant three tier roof, the single bay portico that encircles the building on the outside, the lack of windows, and the protruding *mihrab* on the western side." (Wahby 2007, 51) The symbolism of the mosque remains strong, as the saints are a great source of pride for the nation and for all the Muslims of Indonesia.

The original mosque, Masjid Agung, was built in 1479. As noted in the translation of the *Babad Jaka Tingkir*[15] by Nancy Florida, the mosque is oriented to a true north–south axis. It should be seven degrees north of the west for an accurate *qibla* wall. Some may say this was a miscalculation but if the poems are to be trusted the mosque was deliberately aligned due west of the main public square (*alun-alun*). This maintained the ideal Majapahit planning with a north–south or mountain–sea alignment. Orientation of the mosque towards Makkah would have ruptured this north–south axis. The layout of a central plaza with a mosque to the west and palace to

---

15. There are numerous *Babad* history manuscripts. This one is called by Florida: "a unique history of Java around the turn of the 16th century". It was written in the 19th century in a poetic form by a man who Florida considers a "prophetic" poet. She discovered this series of poems of the *Babad* in the library of the Surakarta Palace.

One of the carved stone columns at the large veranda of Masjid Agung Demak

the south can be found in all the royal Javanese cities. "The Demak Mosque, while accepting Islam did not want to submit to the authority of Islam's Meccan center. Instead, it seeks to define its own version of Islam and set itself up as a center of power from its position at the margins of the Islamic world." (Kusno 2010, 214) Florida has beautifully translated the saga of the creation of the Demak Mosque: "an intricate dialogue between the Middle Eastern Islam and the Javanese religious cosmology. What is interesting is that the negotiation between these two worlds was inscribed in the form and space of the Demak Mosque." (Kusno 2010, 212)

The eastern facade of the mosque faces a large pavilion, serambi, with its own one-tiered hipped gable roof. The eight main pillars are commonly known as Majapahit columns, because they display carved motifs of the Majapahit Empire that was slowly fading as new Islamic kingdoms rose. The columns sit on the traditional stone base—the

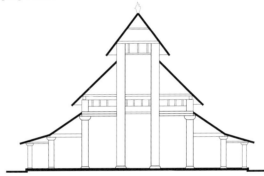

Cross section of the mosque, showing the grand centre columns that reach from floor to the top-tier roof

umpak—here made of a rich black volcanic stone. Many of the older wooden columns repeat the motif of four-sided timber that ascends to eight-sided and then back to four-sided (common also in Malabar). All joints between the vertical posts and horizontal beams are mortise and tenon.

A large undated pair of drums (one vertical and one horizontal) graces one corner of the pavilion. A peculiar detail of the Javanese pavilions and mosque is the junction of the main roof with the pavilion roof. Here, in the interior, amidst the rich carvings and roof details, the large gutter that drains the east mosque roof and west pavilion roof forms the junction between the two roofs. Both roofs have descended to an eave. Ingenuity was required to make this joint functional for rainwater disposal. This detail appears at many older mosques and reminds us that these mosques were originally built as simple squares with no grand front entry pavilion.

Masjid al-Aqsa[16] Kudus (Masjid Menara Kudus)

Another popular pilgrimage site is Demak's neighbouring town, Kudus, a tiny city packed with pilgrims, vendors, beggars, cars, buses and carts. People come in caravans, by bus, minivan and car. The Kudus neighbourhood is a remnant of old Java, with fine wooden houses lining a labyrinth of tiny alleys formed by plaster-covered brick walls. Looking in, one sees houses, courtyards, pavilions, and private gardens. Throughout the town, the sounds of chants, ice cream vendors, boom boxes, children, cars, and horns permeate the senses, along with the scents of Kudus chicken, local cakes and *kopi*.

The mosque complex is enclosed by brick walls, pierced by a series of gates (*gapura*). Directly inside the wall sits a large brick *candi*. In this elaborate structure, the mosque drum is stored. Instead of a minaret for the call to prayer, Kudus has a drum tower. The tower closely resembles brick sanctuaries and gateways of the Majapahit kingdom. The mosque is built around large old brick portals. Founded in 1549 by Sunan Kudus, the structure has little of its original integrity. But the total ensemble

A small neighborhood mosque in Kudus, reached through one of the many narrow lanes of the town

of mosque, tower, and cemetery is notable for the brickwork and the display of pre-Islamic forms. At this compound we once again find Chinese ceramic plates inserted into the brickwork.

The visitors to Kudus are all aimed towards the Tomb of Sunan Kudus, one of the much loved *wali*. Located west of the mosque, the tomb is visited by pilgrims twenty-four hours a day. They come in groups and settle into one of the little pavilions around the tomb. There they chant and sing, preparing for the final moment when they reach the tomb. Series of gates funnel the crowds towards

---

16. al-Aqsa refers to the historic mosque in Jerusalem.

A decorated brick wall and gate at the Kudus site. All visitors reach up to touch the carved wooden lintel.

the tomb. At every gate, the people reach up and children are lifted in order to touch the carved wooden lintel. The carved lintel is scaled to the size of a man with arm upraised—ready for the touch of the people, who have come on their day off to pray.

Kudus, Gala Tembayat (a complex dedicated to the tomb of another *wali*, Sunan Bayat) and Imogiri (a royal tomb) are "a series of architectural elements—mosque and sequential walled courts with ceremonial gateways focusing on the tomb of a saint—are aligned from east to west....The gateways giving access to the sequence of concealed courts are in the form of *candi bentar* and *gapura*, the traditional gateways to Javanese pre-Islamic sanctuaries,…" Pilgrims, who believe there is spiritual benefit to be had from a visit, "…habitually travel to these sacred sites in search of enlightenment in times of adversity." (O'Neil, in Frishman *The Mosque* 236) The tombs

A partial view of the hilltop mosque and tombs at Imogiri. This mountain site is the royal resting place.

are often located at high spots, giving the pilgrims a sense of mission as they climb up an impressive series of steps. As in Sumatra, the link continues between high places, the volcanic mountains, and spiritual inspiration.

Jepara was the main port for the Maluku Islands, thus enormous quantities of nutmeg and cloves passed through this town. Today the area is dedicated to wood carvers and fabricators. Jepara, "carving town", now supplies most of the teak furniture sold in America and Europe. Large container trucks rumble in and out of the town, warehouses are stuffed with teak tables, chairs and miscellaneous furniture. Jepara has moved from nutmeg to teak tables.

In Mantingan, the town just south of Jepara, a large complex of mosque and tomb is found. Here, the classic brick walls and a series of elaborate gateways mark the entry and the passage to the cemetery. The gates, walls and portals are direct descendants of the *candi*. The mosque is locked up and unwelcoming, but the tomb is open and people are praying and offering money, flowers, and papers. Makan Ratu Kalinyamat holds the tomb of the Queen—and her consort, children, and relatives—at least eight graves. From the mosque, facing Makkah, one faces the tombs.

The large old cemetery, with its mosque and tomb complex was officially built in 1559, and completely rebuilt in 1927. Some say it was built by Sultan Hadlirin, husband of Queen Kalinyamat, but probably not, since he died first and the queen ruled until she died in 1579. The old brick walls are definitely from the 16th century but everything else has been rebuilt. The shape and form of the original mosque appears to have been conserved, but materials and finishes are new. Original carved medallions have been set in a new plaster wall. The stonework reflects a strong carving tradition dating back over 500 years. Today, carving has moved from stone to wood. The carvings are similar to ancient floral and lotus forms that are seen in many of the batik motifs. These designs reappear often in the island mosques.

Tomb of the 16th-century Queen Kalinyamat and her relatives

One of the many gates at the mosque and tomb complex at Mantingan

Inland: Kotagede, Surakarta, and Yogyakarta

In the mid-16th century Islam's path of conversion moved inland. The Muslim head of Demak came to Laweyan[17] and made the first inroads into the Majapahit Hindu-Buddhist kingdom. Laweyan was founded in 1546, marking the beginning of the transformation of the Javanese heartland into an Islamic kingdom. Raden Trenggana, the man who brought Islam to Laweyan, was a son of the founder of the Demak kingdom. The influence of the Demak court and Sunan Kalijaga is very visible in Yogyakarta and Surakarta. But, before those two major city kingdoms were created, the Mataram Sultanate began in Kotagede.

Kotagede

Masjid Agung Mataram was originally built in the late 16th century. The town of Kotagede was established as the first seat of the Islamic Mataram Sultanate. As in Cirebon, the town was laid out to encompass the four key components of planning: palace, mosque, town square and market.[18] The

---

17. Kampung Laweyan is a village that forms a part of Surakarta. Small streets with lovely wooden and plaster houses form a labyrinth with alleys displaying batik cloth, cloth makers and dyers.
18. Kotagede Heritage District, Jogja Heritage Society, 2007.

Prayer hall at the Kotagede grand mosque with radiating wood rafters supporting the tiered roof

The gracious veranda at the mosque

The moat encircling three sides of the veranda

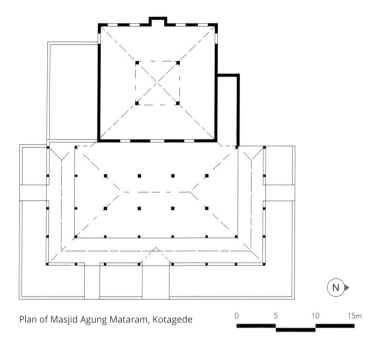

Plan of Masjid Agung Mataram, Kotagede

0   5   10   15m

palace was the centre of governance and house of the king, the market the centre of economic activities. Of these original four, only the mosque and the market survive. The kingdom changed and the seat of government was moved long ago. Kotagede is now a village ruled by Yogyakarta. It remains unique for its beautiful traditional houses, lovely lanes, and the memories of once famous craftsmen, including a thriving silver centre. Considering the intense development of Java and an earthquake in 2006, it is especially gratifying to be able to walk the lanes of Kotagede and have the chance to appreciate the fine craftsmanship shown in the woodwork of the houses. Although the earthquake caused considerable damage to the ancient structures, there is still much to appreciate. The community has made a massive effort to protect and restore the wooden homes.

The mosque prayer hall is a fifteen-meter square with four magnificent teak columns supporting the classic tiered wooden roof. The unpainted square columns at both prayer hall and veranda sit on carved black basalt bases. A large veranda graces the east side of the mosque and leads to the walled courtyard. A water course surrounds three sides of the veranda. Since everyone removes their shoes before entering the mosque, the tradition was to then step into the water, thus cleansing one's feet.

Both veranda and courtyard are typically populated by children, adults and visitors. Merchants from the nearby public market come to relax, sleep, and meet friends. The walls around the complex are brick and stone, reminiscent of traditional Javanese temple compounds. Gates leading out to the neighbourhood do not line up with the mosque so they may be remnants from another time. The tomb of Senopati, one of the early rulers of the Mataram Sultanate, sits in the graveyard to the west of the mosque.

Masjid Agung Surakarta

The grand mosque compound was constructed between 1757 and 1768. As people enter the compound, they move through a series of defined spaces that transport them from the busy street to the inner hall. At the entrance to the royal mosque the roof swoops down to a humble, human-sized height at the eave. The open pavilion roof rises from exterior short squat masonry columns to interior wood columns that support the exposed structure and high open ceiling. From the pavilion one passes into the 34 metre square prayer hall where giant wood columns soar to a series of

tiered roofs. Light pours in from the clerestories between roof layers. The majestic inner four columns are round, braced by horizontal ties connected with delicately worked metal bands. The choice of blue for the veranda of the mosque is magnificent, especially as a contrast to the rich wood tones of the prayer hall structure and ceiling panels. The pavilion's blue wooden columns sit on black stone bases.

The complex includes other buildings, including a pavilion for the *gamelan* in the east courtyard

The prayer hall at Masjid Agung Surakarta

The grand veranda at the royal mosque—Masjid Agung Surakarta

Cross section of the mosque and veranda

Detail of a connection at one of the prayer hall columns

and a bathing/washing annex. The porch veranda embraces the square mosque; it in turn is surrounded by a moat, once used for foot cleansing but now dry. The mosque is full of people resting or reading, children playing and men praying. The Surakarta royal centre of *alun-alun*, mosque and palace are laid out to allow for a true orientation of the mosque *qibla* wall, thus all of the structures are several degrees off true north.

The establishment of this mosque is associated with the transfer of the capital city to Surakarta on February 17, 1745. Sri Pakubuwono II immediately set up a palace and town square but did not have time before his death to build the grand mosque. The majestic new Grand Mosque was constructed during the reign of Sri Pakubuwono III (1749–88). Further renovations were undertaken in 1794 and 1850, including the addition of a minaret.

Masjid Agung Yogyakarta is the palace mosque built in 1773, after two separate kingdoms were established, with Surakarta the home of the Sunan[19] and Yogyakarta the Sultan. The two Agung mosques are very similar and display the 18th-century evolution of the original Javanese mosque. Most fortunately, they both retain the original high open ceiling and have not been closed off like Demak. The full glory of the roof structure is visible, along with beautifully detailed wood columns rising up to the third roof tier.

The mosque follows the traditional Javanese mosque form with a square plan for the prayer hall and a three-tiered roof. A large veranda pavilion graces the east side of the prayer hall and has a two-tiered roof. This rectangular structure connects to the main entry gate with a covered walkway. The compound is walled with several entry gates, the most dramatic facing the main public square. The mosque has been built up over time, starting with the prayer hall, then the verandas and walkways. Several renovations have been undertaken with special attention paid to ensuring that the structure is earthquake resistant.

The prayer hall rises up 1.7 metre above ground level. It is reached through a series of ascending platforms. The courtyard sits a step above the main road, with an ascent to the veranda and finally the steps to the prayer hall. Inside the prayer hall a collection of round pillars supports the roof structure. The four *soko guru* timbers soar 16 meters to the highest central roof. Although all of

The impressive prayer hall at the Masjid Agung Yogyakarta

---

19. Officially, the ruler of Yogyakarta is the Sultan, Sunan refers to the ruler of Surakarta, referring to someone honoured and respected. Sunan is used for all of the *wali songo*.

these teak columns have rich carvings at the tops, below they are smooth and without decoration. In contrast, the columns in the veranda are elaborately decorated and painted with all the royal symbols of the nearby palace. The mosque is well-cared for and recent earthquake upgrades are subtler than the steel cages of Cirebon.

As in the poem about Demak, here too there appears to have been a struggle regarding the orientation to Makkah. Today, all the rugs in the prayer hall run at an angle to the walls and columns. Strips of tape have been placed on the tile at the veranda. Thus, when praying the people do not directly face the *mihrab*, which is not truly oriented to Makkah but aligned on the royal north-south. This struggle continued into the 20th century when Masjid Soko Tunggal (a mosque with a single central pillar) was built on a true north-south orientation. Both these mosques were designed by Yogyakarta palace architects and built by the reigning Sultan, one in the 18th century and the other in 1972. The Javanese traditional layout

The main doors to the prayer hall, Masjid Agung Yogyakarta

of public square, royal residence and mosque followed a strict north-south orientation. The mosque sat to the west of the main public square. Depending on the strength of the royal family, the mosque followed a true north-south (*mihrab* facing due west), or followed the orientation required by the actual location of Makkah.

The mosque courtyard is a popular play-area for local children. A pool channel runs on three sides of the mosque, one side is used as a community wash area and toilet facilities are available. The front pavilion is a well-used meeting point.

Yogyakarta is the bustling capital city of the Yogyakarta Region with a metropolitan population of almost four million. The palace area, which includes the palace, the main *alun alun* and the royal retainer neighbourhood, is surrounded by the remnants of the original palace walls. Here, life moves at a different pace. There are peaceful lanes, open areas, and pavilions for sitting and relaxing. The Sultan's retainers lived along these lanes and practiced their arts, as musicians, dancers, craftsmen and barbers, soldiers and maids. The famous Water Palace built by the Sultan around the time of Masjid Agung is a glory of fantasy. Another structure of the same time is the tiny all masonry Masjid Selo. Both these constructions reflect the influence of the colonial European powers, employing plaster and stone to create patterns, arches and enclosures.

The Yogyakarta royalty built a series of mosques in the surrounding countryside. These 'Pathok Negoro' mosques had special status with royalty in that the villagers (often religious functionaries of the kingdom) paid no tax on their land. They were considered a pillar of the sultanate and were supposed to support the sultan politically and religiously. They also guarded the royal territories of the kingdom. Two of these mosques, Dongkelan and Ploso Kuning, retain much of their original integrity. Dongkelan houses a fine collection of *mustaka*, the finials that have crowned the roof over the centuries of the mosque's life.

Comparisons

"When Islam arrived in Indonesia, it did not cause a revolution in building styles; instead, the architecture of the transitional period (14th-16th centuries) reflected new ideas and influences from a variety of sources but retained fundamental traits from previous eras; Just as Indian ideas had been filtered through an Indonesian screen, so too with Islam and its attendant architectural forms." (Miksic, in *Indonesian Heritage: Architecture*, 86)

The mosques discussed in this chapter are notable for their integrity and for their role in the history of the growth of Islam in Java. The mosques illustrate the path of Islamic conversion and the royal response. Some mosques remain the vibrant centre of the community, others are empty, locked, abandoned or cut off from their

Wooden houses in Kudus, with the fanciful figures of the *wayang* decorating the ridge

The traditional drum in a place of honour on the veranda of the grand mosque of Cirebon

forms are uniquely Javanese and differ from the residential styles (also unique to their region) seen in Sumatra.

On both islands, the mosque evolved from local forms used in house, pavilion or meeting hall. A square floor plan and hipped roof expanded to meet the needs of a congregation and a desire to mark a 'high' point. In the *surau* of Sumatra and the meeting halls of Java, the idea of roof tiers had been utilized before the arrival of Islam. Repeatedly, vernacular religious architecture displays the human need to create a high point to mark spiritual spaces.

The typology of post and beam frame guided mosque construction. Even though the prayer hall has walls, they serve only as guardians for the columns which are the supporting members. Early Javanese mosque compounds displayed elaborate brickwork and gates that harkened back to the preceding Hindu empire. The craftsmanship of the brick entries echoes features of the Hindu/Buddhist monuments still standing throughout the island.

The royal mosques of Java have none of the Sumatran swooping roofs, although the three-tier roof remains popular on both islands. Most royal mosques have round interior columns (except for Kotagede which has only square supports), much like the majority of the Sumatran mosques. Many of the verandas and exterior porches have square supports. The round interior wood posts are left bare or polished, the square timbers are often painted. Since mosque prayer halls were built first, it may be that timbers were still coming directly from the forests, as was the case with the old

neighbourhood. The compounds offer areas for praying, soccer matches, games, bicycle races, washing, swimming, drink and food stalls. There are mosques that face Makkah and ones that don't; mosques with no columns, one column, or a forest of columns. Mosques are sited on hills reached by networks of stairs and steps or sit flatly adjacent to royal palaces.

At many sites, the mosque is surrounded by lanes of traditional Javanese houses, with steep tile roofs, open pavilions, and a raised floor. In Kudus, neat little homes are topped by *wayang*[20] ridge tops. In many towns, the rich are buying up the old wooden houses and reassembling beams and joists, wood post to stone base. Carved beams, doors, screens, posts, vents, overhangs, and ceilings are being restored. The Javanese house has distinctive roof profiles that reflect status. These

---

20. *Wayang* refers to the Javanese shadow puppets. Forms of characters are reproduced as roof-top elements.

Sumatran mosques. With the addition of porches and verandas in the 19th century, the available timbers would have been milled.

In Java, the royal mosques were part of a larger complex. The processional nature of Javanese sacred traditions continued into the Islamic compounds. A series of walls and gates provided a transition from public space to sacred, unlike the Sumatran mosque typically standing alone. The Sumatran mosques had no need for gated walls, for they served as the open centres of village life.

Many of the mosques now have a minaret, but not originally. The tower at Kudus is not really a minaret, but a home for the *bedug*. The form clearly follows ancient Majapahit construction. Moving into later centuries, the influence of Arabia and India brought the minaret. But the people held on to their tiered roofs and open platforms; only in the 20th century do we see the arrival of the 'international' mosque. Instead of the minaret, the Javanese had the *mustaka*, the crown of the tiered roofs, and the drum, *bedug*, which was a part of the *gamelan* and formerly called people to prayer. Throughout Sumatra and Java, both elements remain.

It is worth noting the two major differences between the mosques of the Malabar Coast and those of Indonesia. First, the Indonesian mosques are open to all, women and children are ever present. In Kerala, the mosques are exclusively male. Second, in Indonesia there is tremendous pride in the *masjid tua*, the traditional Indonesian mosque. No one is speaking of demolishing a heritage mosque, there is no embarrassment about the connections between the Hindu/Buddhist past and the Islamic present. The Malabar mosques are vulnerable on many fronts, both their wooden structure and their connection to the Kerala heritage. In India, this is a direct reflection of religious divisions. In Indonesia, Islam is the major faith and connections with the past are noted and studied. The lack of appreciation of the Kerala mosque is in great contrast with the Indonesian pride in their ancient mosques.

A journey following the movement of Islam could move out further, into the Moluccas and beyond. The square, multi-roofed mosques can be found throughout the archipelago. Hopefully, future research will document more of these mosques. Throughout Indonesia there remains a wealth of traditional mosques. Their future is more secure than in Kerala but their integrity is endangered. Solid walls enclose structures, plaster and tiles cover old wood; arches, domes and minarets are added, expansive pools are reduced.

Merchant's Mosque
A Foot in Two Worlds

—————◦⌐————

"Like the Mediterranean, the Indian Ocean functioned since days immemorial, as a great bazaar for the exchange of both goods and ideas."

Marcinkowski (in Karim 2009)

"No country is ever too full for another mosque....foreigners arrived in increasing numbers, and new societies formed as a result of their intercourse. In Calicut, ... the Zamorin hosted four thousand foreign Muslim traders in the fourteenth century, while Muslim Melaka in the fifteenth century hosted many Indian merchants from Cambay, Calicut, and the Coromandel coast, who became officers of the Malay court and some of the wealthiest merchants."

Ho 2006, 57 & 100

"From one end of Islam's world connections to the other, speculators unstintingly gambled on trade...Trade meant towns."
Peak of Islam like Italian renaissance in that "both were based on urban societies enjoying the benefits of trade and riches. ...exceptional people who drew deeply on the ancient civilization ...and who lived centuries ahead of their contemporaries."

Braudel 1993, 71-76

The great ocean crescent of Islam—from Arabia to India and onward to Southeast Asia—was connected by sea trade to everything from gold and tin to spices and cloth. When colonialists took hold of the riches of Asia, the resident merchants initially lost income but they persevered and continued to be engines of local economies. The coastal areas of India and the Indonesian archipelago were never sealed off from each other. The flow of goods, ideas and people was a permanent part of life. Sometimes connections across the sea were stronger than those with fellow inland countrymen. Many of the traders used Bahasa Melayu (the base of today's Malay and Indonesian languages) as the lingua franca of trade.

The mosques of the Indian Ocean littoral were often sponsored by merchants, a practice that continued up to the 20th century. Scattered through the urban landscape these mosques reflected a merchant's pragmatism. They

Wooden sailing ship being built in Beypore. The ancient shipbuilding arts continue to be practised in this town outside of Kozhikode, Kerala.

responded to a need for a prayer hall and reflected the resources of the place. In Kochi, the mosque structure moved towards a variant on the large family home or the godown warehouses; on the Javanese coast the mosques continued to display a distinguished conical roof, but often concentrated in only one grand tier. Mosque design now reflected influences from both local and colonial sources. Merchant mosques in Sumatra and Malaysia were built with masonry walls on a solid foundation floor; builders no longer utilized timber floors and walls. The square plan, a continuance of the original mosque of the Prophet, was favoured. Throughout the littoral, the wood-framed pyramid roof and graceful verandas endured. The all-timber mosque slowly disappeared.

The merchant mosque-builders discovered the minaret. A round or octagonal minaret was placed next to the square prayer hall. These geometric forms were set amidst the dense labyrinth of the port cities. The tall minaret rose separate from the mosque and higher than the mosque roof. A series of openings in a crowning circular room allowed the muezzin, after climbing the stairs, to issue his call. Some minarets even had a tiny balcony circling the top room so that the call to prayer could be issued with no restrictions between the human voice and the surrounding air. Today, loudspeakers blast out the once mellifluous calls and no one climbs the tower stairs. All the Southeast Asian minarets look vaguely like lighthouses, guiding humans through the storm

Minarets in Java. On the left is Semarang, on the right, Pekalongan.

of life by calling them to prayer. In fact, several historians have noted specific mosque minarets as beacons for sailing ships.

In this chapter we will examine 19th-century mosques of Arab, Malay, Indian and Chinese traders, batik makers and sellers, spice wholesalers, merchants and workers. These mosques continued to reflect the specifics of place, including the use of locally sourced materials. At the same time, European colonialists and Muslims returning from the hajj appropriated images from the Middle East and northern India. They encouraged this imagery for any representation of Islam. By the 20th century, this slow chipping away at the native vernacular resulted in an imitation style. Minarets sprouted at every corner, domes proliferated, and marble or tiled surfaces dominated, along with a concrete structure.

Kochi, Kerala, India
Cutchi Hanafi Mosque

Overflowing with trucks, carts, pedestrians, head-carriers, bicycles, motorbikes and cars, Bazar Road links Fort Cochin to Mattancherry. Bazar Road was the heart of the 'native' part of town, the bustling 'bazaar' of the region. Here a great mix of people resided: Arabs, Gujaratis from the north, Tamils from the east coast, Afghanis, Pakistanis, traders from Bombay, Christians and Jews from the Middle East, and, of course, Malayalees. At the southern terminus of Bazar Road sits a complex that includes the Maharaja's Palace and a Hindu temple. Within a kilometre radius can be found Hindu temples, numerous mosques, a Jain temple, a Jewish synagogue, a Catholic church, Syrian Christian shrine, and Kochangadi, the Muslim medieval quarter. All of the diverse people of Mattancherry were brought together repeatedly during years of living and working in close proximity. Over time, immigrant groups assimilated the ways of Kerala and those of their fellow citizens into their own customs. Everyone became less exclusive or self-defined and more cosmopolitan.

Godowns full of rice, rubber, spices, cashews, hardware, and plastic goods line the street and stretch eastwards to the water and the port. Delineating the east edge of the roadway are grand warehouses with imposing double doors leading to expansive courtyards which extend to the water's edge. For centuries this was a place of exchange, a locus for movement of people and goods, a hub for the products that had propelled men to voyage great distances. Kochi became a marketplace for the desired goods of peoples from Beijing to Amsterdam. Today, looking at the empty wharves it is hard to imagine that once this waterway was packed with boats. Even thirty years ago, one could 'walk' the water's edge by jumping from one boat to another.

In the midst of this linear, dense street-front, mosques can be reached through lanes between shops. Here the men of the community, just meters away from their work, have a place to pray or rest. For the most part, the mosques of Bazar Road are more recent than those of Kochangadi. Bazar Road developed into what we see today in the late 18th and early 19th century. The British had established themselves, Gujarati merchants were building permanent warehouses, and the volume of trade was increasing. Here we can see the next stage in the mosque development, reflecting new influences from both the Gujaratis

View of backwater boats arriving at a market, Kerala, in the 19th century

and the Europeans. Arched openings and fanlight windows were integrated into the Kerala model; the Kerala roof held steady, along with the use of local construction methods.

Perched on the western edge of India's Gujarat state, the district of Kutch sits on the Pakistan border. An arid terrain, the land is flanked by salty marshes and the Arabian Sea. From here, many men set out to sea. Known for their trading abilities, Gujaratis had contacts in Arabia, China and throughout India. Gujarati textiles were sought after throughout the Middle East and Southeast Asia, where they were even used as a medium of exchange for spices.

From the early trading days of Kochi, there has been a Gujarati presence. Part of that large community includes the Kutchi[1] (Sunni Gujaratis)

1. The Cutchi mosque is one of the few in Kochi that follows the Hanafi school of law, Kutch being in Gujarat in northern India.

and the Jain Gujaratis who speak the Kutchi dialect. It is said that the King of Cochin offered land for settlements (as he did to the Jewish community) to the Kutchi Memons (or Cutchi Memons as they are known in Kochi) because of their renowned trading abilities.

Tradition has it that in 1819 a massive earthquake hit the Kutch region. The fertile agricultural land became laden with salt, the freshwater disappeared. At this time, a huge migration from Kutch occurred. The majority moved to Bombay (now Mumbai) or to Kochi, places known through their longstanding trade connections.

Since their arrival in Kochi, the Cutchi have prospered; there are now over 3,000 community members. Besides trading in spices and cloth, they were successful in 'transshipment', importing and exporting goods from Kochi. They also branched out into seafood, hotels, and construction. In 1898, they established the Indian Chamber of Commerce. Known for their philanthropy, the Cutchi have founded charitable trusts to fund schools, healthcare, and orphanages. They also own sizeable amounts of property on Bazar Road where they continue to subsidize rent for many marginal businesses. The community originally lived only around Bazar Road, but since the 1950s they have spread throughout greater Kochi so that now there are 18 Cutchi mosques.

In 1815, the Cutchi Memon community decided to build a mosque on Bazar Road. Stories suggest settlement before this date, there may have been a first mosque with a thatch roof. But the mosque

Bazar Road and the entrance to the Cutchi Hanafi Mosque, Kochi

that we see today was built between 1815 and 1825. The first imam of the present mosque was Haji Ibrahim Bawa, a Sufi scholar who came from Gujarat in the early 19th century. The mosque was built by Haji Dosal Kadwani Sait, a successful Cutchi merchant. It is now managed by an organization—Cutchi Memon Jamath[2], which also owns several adjacent properties. The rent from these shops and buildings is utilized for the operation of the mosque.

An arched entry gate leads from hectic Bazar Road down a small lane to the peaceful compound of the Cutchi Mosque. The original mosque is a 14-metre square two-storey structure with a large hipped roof that forms a pyramid-like crown. The building displays elements of the local vernacular

2. The Memons are descendants of the Lohana community of Sindh who converted to Islam; those who settled in Kutch were called Cutchi Memons.

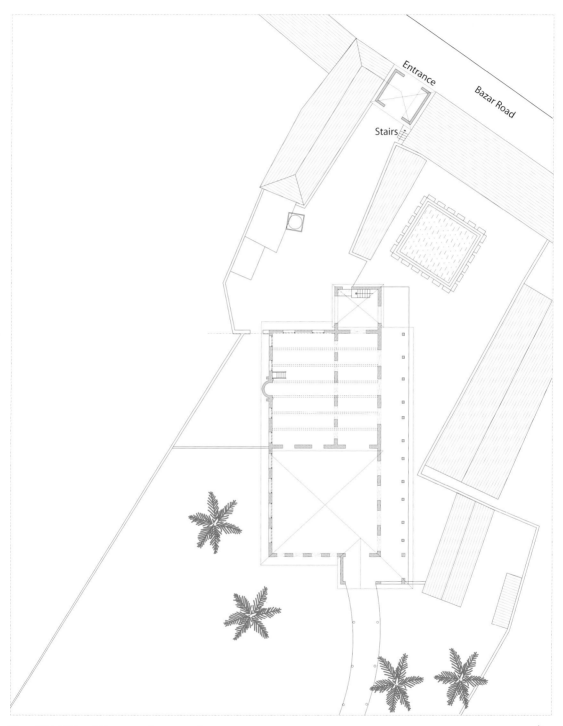

Entrance

Bazar Road

Stairs

Plan of Cutchi Hanafi Mosque and compound.

0 1 2 3 4 5   10m

N

Exterior of the mosque from the entry lane

and relates directly to a class of formidable street-front warehouses lining Bazar Road, although the detail and ornamentation is much more refined in the mosque. Many of the extant Bazar Road structures were built in the early 1800s by Guajarati merchants to replace the thatch huts which previously lined the road.

The prayer hall is a single room with no columns, extending into a generous entry hall through five large arched openings. Two archways at the south open into the 1840 addition, a square one-storey structure for burial functions. The designer of the mosque incorporated elements from the Kutch vernacular: the prevalence of arches and the curved plaster details remind worshipers of their homeland. Elegant carved four-panel doors are a profusion of ovals; this oval is then repeated as one single element on the inside of the wood shutters, a favoured detail from Kutch repeated on many of the Bazar Road warehouses. The *mihrab* arch displays a cornucopia of leaf and flower designs rendered in plaster. The level of detail confirms the presence of skilled artisans who were found to work with the resident craftsmen. After the massive 2001 earthquake in Kutch destroyed many ancient buildings, some say these details can now only be found here.

Six substantial wooden beams close to eight metres long span across the prayer room. The original glass bell jars which held candles still hang from the beams, along with their successor candelabra. Openings to the exterior have fanlights with coloured glass above wooden shutters. The glass is believed to be original; a mix of blue, green, red and clear panes set into the fanlight frame. The wooden balusters at the lower portion of the window openings are made in the classic Kerala style as is the exterior eave board. From the outside, the rounded bay formed by the arched interior *mihrab* can be seen on the *qibla* wall.

The upstairs space is completely open and presently unused. This space has balustered openings in the floor and a small *mihrab* for the overflow crowd that formerly utilized the second floor. The wooden tie beams and roof structure are exposed and replicate the ubiquitous Kerala roof. The steepness of the roof creates an expansive, prominent presence, calling out the public function of the building.

Qibla side of the mosque

Ablution pool

Unlike the older mosques of Kochangadi, there is not a covered veranda with columns surrounding the building, but instead a braced overhang roof at the first floor. Off the entry hall, a veranda with wood columns extends along the entire southeast side of both prayer room and burial space. There is an expansive ablution pool (almost eight meters square) adjacent to the veranda. At the east corner of the mosque a two-storey tower serves as entry, foot pool, and stair for the second floor.

Shophouse arcade, Penang

The entry and veranda floors are of granite pavers. These, along with several large water holders each carved from a single piece of granite, were all imported from the Kutch region. One stone vessel sits adjacent to the ablution pool, three sit along the entry path, adjacent to the old well and a series of vaulted 'bathing' rooms. Long ago, water from the well would be placed in the stones for bathing. An assistant would pour water over the bather, sometimes also heating the bath water.

The compound is large, with an extensive unbuilt area set aside for burial. Besides the Bazar Road entry, a path to the west leads to a residential area. Coconut palms proliferate, providing generous shading around the building and cemetery area. Surrounded on all sides by the densely built up area of Mattancherry, the mosque compound is truly an oasis.

Penang, Malaysia
Masjid Melayu Lebuh Acheh

> "Kampung Masjid Melayu Acheen Street is without doubt the most important historic urban Muslim settlement in Malaysia today in view of the fact that it was once a leading centre of the spice trade in Southeast Asia, a regional hub for hajj travel, Malay press and literature, the Pan-Islamic movement and the religious knowledge network." (Lubis, 92 (Karim 2009)

Early Malaysian mosques were built in a style similar to the Sumatran mosques surveyed in an earlier chapter. Few of these 18th-century timber mosques have survived. But a scattering of the sheltering roof mosques remains; one proud survivor sits in Penang, on the west coast of peninsular Malaysia. Founded by a pepper trader from royalty in Aceh, the mosque and the surrounding compound of traditional houses dominate the neighbourhood. This mosque is included here because it typifies the next generation of mosques in both Sumatra and Malaysia and is a fine example of the close connections between merchants on the two coasts bordering the Straits of Malacca. Only the vagaries of colonialism kept these two lands apart. Despite their overwhelming commonalities the British ruled one side, the Dutch the other. This led eventually to two separate nations.

Lebuh Acheh was the centre of the Malay traders from Aceh, the north coastal area of Sumatra. Penang and the Malay Peninsula were deeply connected with Sumatra, especially Aceh, and the expansive trade between India and China. The street was part of an old Malay *kampung* (or village) in the original George Town settlement. The English naval officer Francis Light had established a settlement on the Island of Penang in 1786 after negotiating a treaty with the Sultan of nearby Kedah. Penang, like the ports along the Malabar Coast, was a landing place for settlement by European colonialists. On Penang Island we find the same confluence of winds and cultures, a place for time spent resting, trading, and waiting for the next monsoon wind.

Penang's relationship with the British shares certain similarities with the history of Malabar. Although the British hoped to leave the Malays, along with the Indian Malabaris, to their own governance, they were also eager to exploit the resources of the land. As the British became more and more involved with the Malay Peninsula, they eventually fulfilled the old Malay proverb: "Once the needle is in, the thread is sure to follow." Edward Said believed that the "Oriental-European relationship was determined by an unstoppable European expansion in search of market, resources, and colonies…" (Said 1979, 95)

The city grew as a multicultural centre of trade in pepper, cloves, nutmeg, camphor, tin, and, increasingly over the colonial years, opium. Settlers came from peninsula Malaysia, India, China, Sumatra, Java, Burma and the Middle East. Penang was typical of many colonial Southeast Asian cities in the intermingling of people from diverse backgrounds and cultures. The historic centre of Penang, George Town, was a dense ensemble of housing, warehouses, shops and religious structures. Over one thousand classic two to three-storey shophouses still stand in the historic centre. These connected rows of structures house businesses on the ground floor and families up above. The second floor extends over a ground floor five-foot walkway (*kaki lima*), thus gracing the old city centre with a continuous arcade. Street fronts of shophouses and block-long arcades define the unique urban character of George Town. In 2008, George Town, along with Melaka, was recognized by UNESCO as a World Heritage Site: Historic Cities of the Straits of Malacca.

Lebuh Acheh abuts a large Chinese community[3] and an adjacent Tamil Indian market centre. Masjid Melayu[4] was founded in 1808 by Tengku Syed Hussain Al-Idid. He is referred to as an Arab

---

3. Just one block away sits the Khoo Kongsi, a spectacular clan temple and theatre compound constructed with a double row of shophouses guarding the entrance.

4. A profusion of terms has been used for the Malay Mosque. Called Masjid and Mesjid, it is sited on Acheen Street or Lebuh Acheh. Malay spelling is Acheh versus Sumatran Aceh.

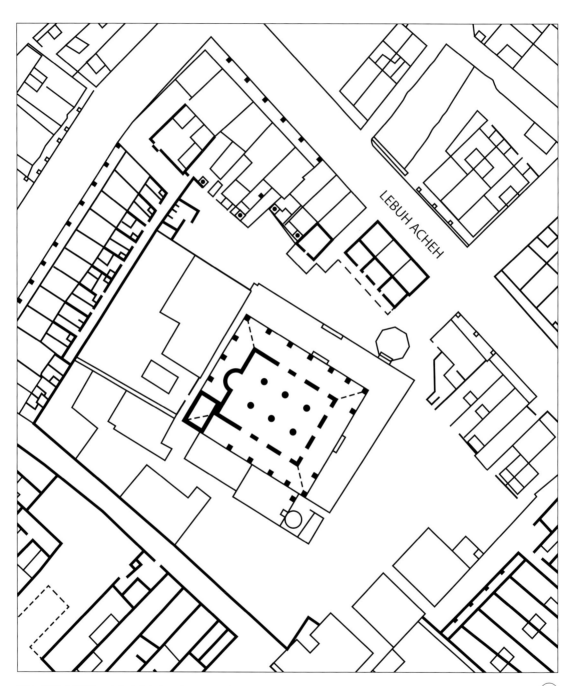

LEBUH ACHEH

Plan of Masjid Melayu Lebuh Acheh and compound

Not to scale. N

merchant prince, but he was from an Acehnese royal family, so his connections are more with Aceh and Sumatra than Arabia. Syed Hussain moved to Penang shortly after the arrival of Light. The two signed a treaty in 1791, with Syed Hussain noted as the leader of the Malay community. He set up an office and godown at the port and was vastly successful as a merchant trading in pepper, rice, betel nut, gold and more. He died in 1826 a rich man; he and his family are buried beside the mosque.

The mosque compound is quite large, enclosed by the adjacent rows of shophouses to the north and east and a loose collection of stand-alone double storey homes to the south. A small cemetery is to the west. Bungalows in the mosque compound reflect the Malay vernacular. Masonry piers support a timber-framed second storey. The top storey is reminiscent of the raised timber *kampung* homes found throughout Sumatra and Malaysia. All of the house ownerships trace back to Sumatrans, except one which was the home of

Entry view of the mosque and minaret

Prayer hall

a Hadhramaut Sufi, Sheikh Omar Basheer, who became the much-revered imam of the mosque until his death in 1881.

The mosque sits an angle to the street to reflect the proper orientation to Makkah. An octagonal minaret stands prominently at the narrow entrance from street to mosque. From the street the mosque is partially obscured by the minaret, which serves as impressive guardian and greeter. A striking vertical element in a landscape of two- and three-storey shophouses, the minaret is a landmark for the neighbourhood. The opening from Lebuh Acheh into the mosque courtyard is similar to the Cutchi mosque in Kochi in that the bustle of the street is moderated as one passes into the mosque compound.

Masonry walls and octagonal columns support the wood-framed roof. The rectangular mosque has a raised base and hipped terracotta tiled roof. Roof hip ridges reflect Chinese motifs common in Penang. The oldest veranda has a sloped roof and surrounds the prayer hall. A more recent veranda extends out to the north and the east. It has a flat roof coming off the original roof eaves. The interior prayer hall has a high flat ceiling. Typical of many of the merchant's mosques, an eclectic collection of arches graces the mosque. An outer wall with Moorish (horseshoe shaped) and Mughal arches was added when the veranda was expanded. In addition to the veranda arcs, the main mosque has large arched openings with fan-shaped transoms. Ornate plaster capitals and cornices have replaced the wood carvings of early Malay/Indonesian mosques. All the masonry walls are brick with lime plaster. A large ablution pool, reminiscent of Kerala, lies to the south.

In 1994, the federal government allocated funds for the conservation of the mosque. Now that the work has been completed the mosque and the compound have been given a renewed life.

Over the years historic mosques were layered with symbols from afar. Around the same time as the construction of Masjid Melayu, the Tamil Indian community of Penang built a mosque of similar style, Kapitan Keling Mosque. As the Indian traders gained wealth, they added elements from India and further afield. The early hipped roof structure gained a series of domes and minarets and a grand elevated entrance. Traces of the original still exist but for the most part the traditional mosque is now only a memory.

Pekalongan, Java, Indonesia

"Observers from the 16th century noticed how little of their wealth Southeast Asians put into houses and other fixed property, and how much into items of dress and bodily decoration." (Reid, 2009, 33)

Pekalongan was a centre of trade, known for its production of exuberant batik and woven fabric. In return for the delectable spices of Southeast Asia, the merchants of India offered high-quality cloth, the barter goods for spices, as early as the 1500s. Cloves and nutmeg, aromatic woods and gold were exchanged for cloth. In fact, cloth was a form of currency until the Dutch introduced coins in their ever-expanding Indonesian colonies.

Cotton grew in Southeast Asia, but quality and quantity of Indian cloth could not be matched. Indian cloth gained prestige when it underwent the Javanese resist dyeing process known as batik—a combination of Chinese and Javanese

Exterior of Masjid Wakaf, Pekalongan

techniques. By 1700, the Javanese were producing enough batik to export and their cloth became a dominant trade commodity. Merchants from throughout the littoral settled in the *Pasisir* to take advantage of the booming trade. Many of these were Muslims from India; eventually they built mosques. Today, Pekalongan, which sits halfway between Cirebon and Semarang, remains a land of pattern: swirls and stripes, dots, leaves, and birds accumulate on lengthy spans of cloth.

Masjid Wakaf[5] (Waqf) stands on Jalan Surabaya in the Arab quarter, a neighbourhood dominated by the batik trade. Here, non-European merchants from around the world established their homes, shops and places to worship. Masjid Wakaf was founded by Said Hussein (Said Husein Atas K.B.Tk Islam Salafiyal). Different documents refer to him as a merchant or a religious leader. All agree that he was from the Hadhramaut and settled in the *Pasisir* in the early 1800s. Arabs from Yemen had been trading with the coast since the 16th century and thus had generations of connections. The influx of Hadhrami Arabs to Java had greatly increased due to disturbances in Yemen from the enforcement of a puritanical Islamic Wahhabism. By the 1850s, fifteen thousand Hadhramis were living in the *Pasisir*.

---

5. Wakaf is an endowment for perpetuity, a gift of property often used for the establishment of a mosque. Income from the endowment is used to fund the ongoing operation of the mosque.

Prayer hall at Masjid Wakaf, Pekalongan

Design of what locals call the 'Arab'[6] mosque reflects the Malabar model—a big room with a flat ceiling, lots of doors, windows, fans and clocks. This 19th-century mosque is a one-storey structure with a gracious veranda circling the prayer hall. The mosque floor is raised and reached by two generous steps. A large high-ceilinged, square prayer room is marked by six sizable columns. The vertical axis of the Javanese prayer hall has been replaced with one more horizontal, albeit lofty. Light and breezes filter in from ample door openings. The main entry has arched transoms above large double doors; two sides continue the double doors but with rectangular transoms. The *qibla* wall has a triple arched *mihrab*.

The building exterior has tall plastered masonry walls and a one-tier pyramid roof. The minaret is round with arched openings at the top where the call to prayer was issued. Today, the five daily calls boom out through loudspeakers, ignoring the graceful minaret and the big drum which is prominently placed on the veranda. A guide states that the drum is in fact used for Ramadan and major holidays.

6. Many of the Arabs were in fact of Indian origin or Muslim immigrants from around the Indian Ocean trade routes.

The classic Javanese tiered roof and *mustaka* at the 19th-century Masjid Agung Pekalongan

Masjid Agung Kauman Pekalongan has a similar prayer hall to Masjid Waqf, with the same high flat wood ceiling and generous columns, albeit on a grander scale. Behind a fake Indo-Islamic front sits the original mosque with a classic three-tiered Javanese roof. At least the original prayer hall has been maintained, but the additions of encircling masonry walls and minaret are reminders of the lack of esteem that plagues the old mosques. The outer veranda does serve as town retreat: a place to sleep, talk, and enjoy the shade. Kids run around, old people lay around. Each person carries out their business, left alone, at peace.

Semarang, Java, Indonesia

Semarang, another of the trading cities on the *Pasisir,* was once the largest port in the Dutch East Indies. From here, abundant agricultural products of the rich Javanese soil, especially coffee, tea, and sugar, made their way to European homes. Today, it is a large industrial centre and the third largest port in Java.

Kampung Melayu[7] housed the men of spices and cloth, a place of merchants and the gateway to the city. The presence of the *kampung* was already noted in the 17th century. The settlement

7. Once again we see a reference to Melayu, an ancient term that refers to the Malay people, principally the people who lived along the Straits of Malacca, both from Malaysia and Sumatra. Some say that the original Malay race migrated to Sumatra and throughout the Malay peninsula. Kampungs, village settlements, are found throughout the island nations, sometimes submerged inside large urban cities. They stand as a surviving remnant of village life.

on the riverbank served as the main connector between the government centre to the south and the port on the Java Sea. The original palace and *alun-alun* have since been cut off by roads from this linear arrangement.

Masjid Layur or Masjid Menara Kampung Melayu stands in a dense neighbourhood of the former fine old homes of merchants, all sinking into oblivion. They sink in two ways: first because of lack of upkeep and second, because like coastal cities as far away as New Orleans or Venice, Semarang is sinking due to a shrinking aquifer. Growth in industry and population caused the authorities to pump water from aquifers underneath urban land. That land is now subsiding, taking with it the old buildings. A reconfiguration of the harbour has multiplied the damage since new port construction changed water courses and increased sedimentation of the river. The level of the adjacent river is now higher than the old city.

The city government redoes the streets so that transport can be on elevated ground, but the old buildings appear lower and lower. Original doorways can be seen, isolated, sitting in wells, way below the street. The drains don't really drain, so during the rainy season the door wells fill and flood, as did the old roadways. The administration—putting a modern face on everything—raised the roadway. Solving the bigger problem of drainage, water pumping and or cleaning up the river remains a task outside the government's interest.

Exterior of Masjid Menara Kampung Melayu, Semarang

Where are the Dutch? The Dutch cleared the cities and countryside of resources, sending tons of gold back to the homeland. They also made sure that rivers and channels drained. Now, the Dutch are gone and the Indonesians have control of their resources (or the government elite does), but the culverts don't empty and the historic centre is endangered.

Masjid Menara Kampung Melayu is watched over by Mr. Ali, the mosque keeper for the last 12 years. The mosque is squeezed onto a small site directly on the river, at the approved Makkah angle, with a round lighthouse-style minaret at the street wall. In fact, the minaret may have been used as a lighthouse, since its river location close to the sea was suitable for guiding ships to the port. Menara in the mosque name refers to the minaret. The mosque was built in 1802 by Arab, Malay and Gujarati descendants who traded textiles as well as great quantities of spices. Nutmeg was brought to this urban neighbourhood of traders to be transported around the world.

The mosque has the traditional three-tiered roof with the top tier an extended pyramid crowned by the ever present *mustaka*. Running around two sides of the exterior a low overhang is supported by steel brackets, probably added at a later date. This overhang shades the windows and provides protection at the entry. There is no front entry hall, but an extension of the overhang provides an odd-angled veranda space on two sides. This extension follows the property line and the river. The angle of the mosque and *mihrab* is accentuated by the property borders and the adjacent buildings. A

series of steps ascends to the raised base and the prayer room. Fortunately, the mosque is elevated for when the river floods the water soars to floor level.

The square prayer hall has a high beamed ceiling with four large timber columns marking the central square. The lofty ceiling is composed of solid wood beams and planks, similar to the grand mosque of Pekalongan. Large shuttered windows with arched tops fill the walls. The lower portion of the plastered wall has been covered with big white bathroom tiles. The exterior wall is also sheathed in tile.

Slowly, the mosques of the spice trade became more uniform. From Malabar to Java and beyond a square floor plan prevailed, columns went from wood to masonry, the tiered roofs, while still dominant, became more subdued. Colonialism reduced the wealth of local communities and brought in influences from around the world. More Muslims made the hajj and came back with ideas of uniformity. The exuberant display of local motifs that early builders embellished in the mosques was tamped down into a standard 'look'. In Kerala, North Indian style mosques dominated; in Indonesia and Malaysia, elements from Arabia, India and Europe appeared, overshadowing the cultural and climate responsive local vernacular. Many of the existing traditional mosques that still stand have been dressed up with encircling walls of arcs, corner minarets, and even domes. For now, should these merchant mosques be seen as a last iteration of the monsoon mosque vernacular or can we look to a new interpretation of this typology?

Conclusion

―――――――⌒――――――

"When a hypothesis is deeply accepted it becomes a growth which only a kind of surgery can amputate. Thus, beliefs persist long after their factual bases have been removed, and practices based on beliefs are often carried on even when the beliefs which stimulated them have been forgotten. The practice must follow the belief. ...The things of our minds have for us a greater toughness than external reality."

John Steinbeck, *The Log from the Sea of Cortez*, 148-149

"...the printed word is so definitive, so testimonial and compromising, that it is difficult to simply release it, without precautions, to the scrutiny of possible readers."

Alvaro Mutis, *The Adventures and Misadventures of Maqroll*, 102

The light and sounds of the monsoon world are intense. The sun can be blinding; the monsoon rains can obscure spatial definition. Experiencing a monsoon mosque, one moves from the penetrating brilliance of the sun to the dramatically contrasting interior shade and shadows. The white light of the shadow-less tropical noon is markedly different from the shaded glow of the interior. The acoustics are sometimes haunting: the call to prayer rising up and over the enormous racket of the street, marketplace and the rain itself.

The stories that come with the mosque encompass tall tales, legends, and deep beliefs. Memories are sometimes of the myth of the past. Some mosques have a shadowy history with many unknowns, others shout out a version of their importance. At every mosque visited, someone would appear, willing to talk and answer questions. Although some information appeared dubious with further study, no one could doubt the sincerity of the speaker, their ability to fold years upward. When asked dates, the answer "years ago" implies the great immense past. "In the end, stories are what's left of us, we are no more than the few tales that persist." (Rushdie 1995, 110)

All of the mosques in this book have long chronicles with uncertain and varied building dates. All have been rebuilt several times. A 16th century date can be expanded back in time to the 14th century; one authority may claim an 18th-century building origin while another puts the construction earlier. Dates in old documents refer to the Malayalam or Javanese or Islamic calendar, rarely the Western. For centuries, there was no written history in much of the Indian Ocean littoral. Even the carved inscriptions can be interpreted in various ways, some are illegible.

All that is known for certain is that the buildings hold many stories. The mosques provide physical evidence of the stories, serving as the material culture or the "stuff" of the forbearers. They are solid proof for the presence of the Muslim trading communities.

Until contemporary times, there was a tradition of continuity of building practices in the East. A temple could be built and rebuilt, maintaining the spirit of the original. Each time, the building was assembled on the original foundation or structure, using the same conventions of construction and materials. The building was an ongoing chronicle. New materials and methods have completely changed this process, resulting in a loss of continuity from ancient building to contemporary structure.

In studying the monsoon mosques, grand theories need to be avoided. In fact, exploring the mosques of the tropics reveals them in all their idiosyncratic glory. Instead of dressing up the old mosques with marble, tile, and plastic roofing there should be an appreciation of their inherent handmade beauty and innate dignity. For many mosques, the original has become lost, a glint in the eye, a hint of former serene days.

A great wind of intolerance has swept across the mellow, laid-back Muslims of South and Southeast Asia. The heterogeneous religion created in situ is being pushed out of villages, towns and cities. The Sufi acceptance of existing customs is now seen as heresy. The Arabian Peninsula, home of traders lauded for their open trade practices in the early centuries, is now the centre of an effort to micro-

Veranda at Masjid Agung, Kotagede

manage all Muslims. With their oil wealth and control of Makkah, these Arabs repeat the colonial disregard for the local traditions of Muslims throughout the Indian Ocean world.

Tim Mackintosh-Smith traced the path of Ibn Battuta back to Malabar to investigate what was left of Battuta's world. His description of the famous "oldest mosque in Malabar" at Cranganore lucidly traces the transformation of Islam from the syncretic religion of 14th-century Malabar to today.

> "The old mosque hadn't been demolished. It had been sheathed in a new, pan-Islamic façade. But why? They were obviously proud of having the oldest mosque in Malabar. Why hide it away beneath carbuncular concrete? ....He patted an enormous bronze lamp, sitting on a small platform...The upper tier was scalloped, each projection designed to hold a wick...It was a gift from one of the Samudari Rajas. We used to light it when the students recite the Holy Qur'an. But not long ago we stopped using it. It is of the same form as the Hindu temple lamps.

> It was then that I saw a glimmer of what might be going on. The temple lamp and the Hindu-style carvings were embarrassing...The mosque, this dark and distinguished beauty, had been put in purdah, clad in a style which wouldn't have looked out of place in any modern Islamic setting from Luzon to Luton. They were proud of its age, but not of the Indian, pagan elements in its ancestry, and going by Faysal's comment on the lamp it had come on recently." (2005, 273-4)

Throughout Malabar the message has been received: no longer can the many connections between Hindu, Muslim, Jew and Christian be left visible. The long history of flexibility and respect appears to have come to an end. In Kerala, once known for its embrace of all religions, times have changed in the last decade. A 'keep out' philosophy has arisen out of an atmosphere of conspiracy and mistrust. The 21st century has seen the rise of fundamentalists (of all faiths), creating an atmosphere of mistrust amongst Indians. One source told me that "those" guys tore down the famous mosque in northern India—why not here? Ignored were the historic facts that the mosques of Kerala were built on formerly unoccupied land and that they had always been mosques. The community no longer talks with pride of the adaptation of the local building traditions.

In Indonesia and Malaysia, both Muslim-majority countries, mosque caretakers openly invite all into the prayer hall. Proud of their mosque, they are eager to describe its secret wonders. In Indonesia, the pride is backed up by ongoing maintenance of the historic mosques, albeit only select famous ones. In Malaysia, there is an acknowledgment of the surviving mosques, but the pervasive attitude is to move on, to new forms and new mosques. Unfortunately, even in these once tolerant countries, a wave of doctrinaire imams has arrived, telling communities that they can no longer honour the founding saints or maintain rituals from a bygone past. The Sufis taught acceptance of difference and coexistence, their beliefs became the basis of the Islam that developed in the archipelago and along the Malabar Coast. Elements of the place and the customs were integrated into Islam. A wave of conversions resulted, coupled with a rich faith. Will this long and fertile tradition continue?

In this present climate of intolerance what role might architectural conservation play? Conservation could become—must become—even more relevant; the old buildings can remind a population of the messy and rich past, of the ability of diverse peoples to benefit from living and working together. If all physical evidence of the past is removed (as the fundamentalists propose in building standardized new mosques), then a powerful result of the peaceful synthesis of Islam into the monsoon world is no longer apparent. The visible reminders of the communal efforts that built on the traditions of the spice-producing kingdoms would be lost. Abandoning the old mosques means erasing the celebration of the rich tropical vernacular. The past has much to teach and the conservation of historic mosques acknowledges an important source of phenomenological recall.

The Arabization of Islam is sadly a misinterpretation of the history of Islam. As Sherban Cantacuzino wrote:

> "How can the separate identities of these cultures – the regionalism of Islam – survive in the face of modern views and methods that seek everywhere to standardize and unify? For the strength of Islam has always lain in unity through diversity – the unity of Islam itself through the diversity of its multifarious cultures." (ed.1985, 11)

Another issue of concern for the survival of the mosques is the ongoing battle over origins. Despite the beliefs of most Javanese and Sumatrans that their mosques came out of local traditions, innumerable theories of foreign origin have surfaced in academic journals, from the Dutch in colonial times to scholars of today. These writers often betray a bias: to prove that local design had little inherent value or confirm a prejudice that only imported design was of value or validate a need to connect a small village with a larger empire. What is especially ironic in these days of subaltern studies and academic push-me, pull-you is the transfer of the colonialist prejudices to the local prejudices. Twentieth-century scholars turned the world of history upside down when they critiqued an author's perspective and saw that where you came from influenced how you processed facts. The concern was that Western scholars' interpretation of the East was biased.

Just as Europeans had huge blind spots, so too do some Asians. Several Indonesian and Malaysian academics have stressed direct Arabic or Chinese origins for both Islam and the local mosque vernacular. Their articles appear to disregard the long history of trade where connections were made (in both directions) from Arabia to India, India to Southeast Asia, Southeast Asia to China. They want to eliminate the middleman. The attempt to cover up the idiosyncrasies of South and Southeast Asian Islam means the removal of the local holy men, the intermarriages, and the slow movement of men, religion and ideas. All the more refreshing then the work of scholars at the Institute of Southeast Asian Studies (ISEAS) and others who have conscientiously attempted to be unbiased in identifying numerous distinct paths to local origins.[1]

---

1. Bambang Setia Budi (2004) has done an excellent job of tracing and summarizing the theories of the origin of the Javanese mosque. See also Shokoohy and the volume edited by Gunawan Tjahjono, *Indonesian Heritage: Architecture*.

Radiating wood rafters at Kotagede mosque. Other examples of this type of structure can be seen at many traditional mosques, including the grand mosques of Surakarta and Yogyakarta.

It is not my place to enter the debate about where and when Islam arrived in Asia, but it is worth elaborating some of the reasons why the theories on a foreign origin of the mosque are flawed. The idea that the Indonesian mosque design came from Chinese origins can be pre-empted by studying temples and structures built by Chinese immigrants in the Southeast Asian archipelago. In Cirebon and in nearby Semarang, one can clearly see the difference between the Chinese-inspired temples and the local mosques. Both cities have long held large ethnic Chinese populations and many Chinese temples. The construction of the temples, especially the methods of placing and joining wood members is strikingly different from the mosques.

Chinese temples are lengthy and rectangular with a centre ridge and a gable at each end; beams run horizontally. The Javanese mosque is square with a pyramidal roof of many tiers and a structure of ascending (vertical) rafters that rise from horizontal beams at each roof tier. Temples built by immigrant Chinese utilized capitals and a bracket support system more than the direct mortise and tenon joints of the mosques. The Chinese place beams one on top of another, whereas the Javanese method is to insert layers, as seen in the old pavilions and houses of Java. The Chinese immigrant craftsmen built their temples utilizing what appear to be Chinese temple traditions.

Some details exist in both mosques and temples, such as the "duck" swoop at the end of ridges. Otherwise, one would have to defer to the clear preference for local design, noting that of course the waves of ideas that came with trade included clay tiles, ceramic plates, carved calligraphy, and later, arched openings. Certainly, Chinese craftsmen were involved in mosque building, and many Muslims were ethnic Chinese. But the guiding inspiration appears to have come from local traditions. In Malaysia, which also has a large, historic ethnic Chinese population, similar

Roof structure at Chinese temple in Semarang

discussions have occurred. The three-tiered roof of the old mosques has led some to the Chinese pagoda, whereas in fact the three-tiered roofs of Javanese, Sumatran and Malaysian mosques are much larger and cubic and follow the ancient pavilion tradition.

Examining the Chinese influence on the mosques one must also remember that Southeast Asians and Malabar Indians are Sunnis who follow the Shafi'i school of law whereas the majority of Muslims in China (and northern India) follow the Hanafi school. A different trade route produced a different school of law. Mark Woodward notes that the Malay texts from both Malaysia and Sumatra "mention that Islam arrived from south India." The Malabar ports were used by traders from Sumatra and Malaya, thus ties between these places were strong. "Similarities of mosque architecture lend additional support…the domed mosques of north India were notably absent in both regions (Indonesia and Kerala) prior to the

nineteenth century. In Kerala, Java, and Lombok the oldest mosques are constructed from wood rather than stone or brick and have triple tiered roofs similar to those of South Asian Hindu and Jain temples." (Woodward 1989, 55)

Considering the pace of urban growth and development in Asia, the monsoon mosques are vulnerable—not only to demolition but also to the loss of their surroundings. The art of conservation is not widely practiced today, nor are buildings seen in a context that acknowledges the role of neighbouring environs, from the palm-treed property and expansive pools to the surrounding houses and shops. Context is important for conservation on many levels. The ongoing viability of the mosque is directly related to the stability of the neighbourhood. The condition of the mosque is a clear indicator of the health of the local population. The mosque cannot stand alone—it needs a community for financial support and for the men's presence at prayer. Change is inevitable, yet there is no reason why the old mosques cannot thrive and adapt to contemporary life. Conservation is not static but a process of renewal. If, in the wider community nothing is being maintained, and everything is new, the practice of conservation becomes an unknown.

Until the early 20th century, mosques were built in the style of the local vernacular and faithfully maintained, even rebuilt. For centuries the old mosques of timber and stone endured, fighting off bugs, mould and rain. Today, ongoing upkeep is irregular. Ancestors were able to maintain these structures (some for over five hundred years) but the modernists have been unable to master the heat, moisture and extremes of the monsoon lands. Tropical architecture has always depended on regular renewal to stall the deterioration of building materials. In the days of the mud hut, a family needed to redo the thatch roof annually or biannually. For bamboo walls, the bamboo panels were replaced frequently. Once plastered walls of stone came into use, they had to be painted and repaired after every monsoon season or mould blackened them. The impermanence of materials necessitated an ongoing system of maintenance. Historic photographs display well-maintained buildings, but today the concept of keeping up old structures is often forgotten. Now, there are countless roofless buildings, mouldy walls and overgrown gardens. As the old crumbles, the new grows and rapidly deteriorates, to be followed by a newer new. Limited lifespan—the notion of planned obsolescence—has become a mantra of the modern age. Too many people believe new construction to be maintenance-free. One only need look at black-streaked, recently constructed concrete facades in countless towns in the tropics to know that all buildings need care.

After World War II and independence for India, Malaysia and Indonesia, the populace emphatically welcomed the new: a new country, new economy, new technology, and new cities. Modern architecture was optimistically promoted. But with time, the global marketplace trivialized modernism with a plethora of cheap materials and poorly thought-out designs. Mosque design turned outward from tropical splendours and began to mimic the styles of Persia, North India, Arabia and beyond. Asia indulged in a universal embrace of the modern style—a style for all, specific to none. There was a rejection of the elegant simplicity of the old mosques. An attempt was made to fill the mosques with glitzy materials. Domes were added, arches of all styles proliferated, floors and walls were marbleized.

Since the advent of inexpensive airplane travel, more and more South and Southeast Asians go on the hajj. In addition, many young workers go to the Gulf States for employment. Upon return home, the workers often give large donations to their local mosque, as an act of devotion and to publicly show that their years of work brought rewards. The haji return with stricter ideas about their faith. Funds (and funders) encourage new construction, either as an addition or a completely new mosque. Old mosques, such as many in Kochi, are torn down and replaced with uninspiring structures.

Additions to the old mosques have seldom complimented the existing structures. In Java and Sumatra, walls are tiled, roofs are covered with metal, pools are filled. In Malaysia, most old mosques no longer exist. In Kerala, new interventions get layered onto the graciously proportioned halls. Everywhere domes, minarets, concrete columns and flat roofs surround the old masterpieces with scant attention to proportion or integrity. Too often the vernacular mosques are seen as deficient in a perceived Islamic 'pedigree'; the great rain-shedding roofs and distinguished prayer halls remain vastly under-appreciated. A three hundred year old prayer hall is a venerable site. It has borne witness to a multitude of very human concerns. Samar Akkach elegantly ponders the role of architecture in Islam in "…the notion of *i'tibar*, the need to reflect and "take lessons" from the events of past generations in order to understand God's hidden wisdom." (Akkach 2005, 150) In a sense this is a universal need. Margaret Visser wrote *The Geometry of Love* about a small church outside Rome. But her thoughts on "constructions in space" resonate for buildings of religion throughout the globe.

> "Such structures can cause us to remember. Their endurance, as well as their taking up space, may counter time and keep memory alive. … If the building has been created within a cultural and religious tradition, it constitutes a collective memory of spiritual insights, of thousands of mystical moments." (8-12)

Time is long overdue to celebrate and acknowledge the role of these places. The old mosques continue an ancient and powerful relationship of home to house of prayer. Perhaps not having put to words the importance of a specific mosque, the faithful should be strongly encouraged to find the vocabulary to express their fondness for a place before it is abandoned. The surviving vernacular mosques are outstanding examples of age-old traditions, all the more remarkable because they are a living heritage, still functional, perfectly climate-engineered, dynamic, and in daily use.

Why conserve? "answer …lies in the paradox… that it is precisely this rapidity of change that increases the psychological need for permanence." Second answer "is the realization

Mosque under renovation on the island of Java. A glimpse of the old drum can be seen along with a portion of the tiered roof.

A historic mosque outside Ponnani, Kerala, with the recent addition to the right. The arches, marble surfaces, flat roof and a concrete dome contrast with the traditional wood gable, carvings and sloped roof.

that the old buildings often do their job better than the new ones." Third "earth's fossil fuels are a finite resource...no one can any longer afford to demolish buildings that are basically sound." (Cantacuzino, ed.1985, 21)

'Climate change' and 'sustainability' are the new buzz words. In fact, building conservation is a major way to reduce the energy expended to construct. Production of concrete[2] and steel consumes enormous amounts of fossil fuel. Reuse cuts out much of the energy costs of building a structure. Additionally, in the hot wetlands of the tropics a minimum amount of energy is consumed inside the old buildings. Since ancient methods of cooling are integral to old structures, there is no need for costly air conditioning systems. Tall structures with louvered walls, verandas, and porous stones (e.g. the laterite of Kerala) are just a few of the early practices that ensured comfortable liveable spaces. In designing and building a large space for gatherings (such as a mosque), it was made as comfortable as possible. Mechanical means were not available, but the task was completed satisfactorily. Our present blindness to the global cost of energy use and our love of technology has debilitated design skills and caused generations of architects to ignore climate-sensitive solutions.

The same could be said about materials. In the past, buildings were constructed with locally sourced materials (brick, stone, timber). This is now a goal of 'green' architecture. Timber has been rediscovered as a relevant (and sustainable)

Looking from the mosque to the village of Pariangan.

structural tool for buildings, including mid-rise structures. Conservation ensures the continued visibility of building traditions that represent a minimal consumption of energy. Certainly, new mosques will continue to be built as populations grow and move. They will not look like the monsoon mosques, but they could use as a guide the body of knowledge embedded in the vernacular while creatively designing new structures.[3]

The challenge for conservation in Asia is to take advantage of modern methods while at the same time following a path that celebrates community consensus over individualism. The people of

---

2. The production of cement is one of the three main contributors to carbon dioxide emissions.
3. The first steps have been seen in the work of the Indonesian Atelier Enam in the design for Said Naum Mosque in Jakarta. The mosque is an elegant contemporary structure with a lightness and openness that responds to the culture and climate of place.

India and Indonesia, deeply rooted in place, have been consistently noted for their cooperation and acceptance/tolerance of others. The Western model of striving for originality and individual expression was not historically a part of Eastern consciousness. Reuse, rebuilding, and communal efforts were a respected part of a community's work. Modernity can and should be modified to fit the history of the East, not be based solely on the West. Indians and Indonesians can select what works for them. Multiple visions of modernity are possible and can form a basis for construction that highlights site-specific responses and variations on traditions.

The purist preservation professionalism of Europe and America may not be a good model for the East. Hands-on endeavours and cyclical thinking are more familiar to the people of Asia. Sacks of money are not required, but a return is needed to the tradition of maintenance and cooperative stewardship. Of course, financial aid for conservation is always appreciated, but if every mosque community waits for someone to come forth with all the funding, the very structures that require care decay further. Every mosque needs community commitment. Trusmi, on the island of Java, is a good example of how a community can come together to maintain historic buildings. When a structure is taken over by a government agency or an NGO it becomes a distant object, an abstract aesthetic, no longer a part of daily life. The beauty of vernacular is its mixed-up, diverse heritage. It does not need purifying, it needs recognition, respect, and a congregation's commitment to upkeep.

At the same time, mosque administrators need counsel on selection of materials and design of additions. Wall tiles, cement plaster and easily obtained metal roofing may be cheap and popular, but they are not always the appropriate answers for repairs at traditional mosques. Although domes and minarets may seem more "Islamic" they may not be the proper addition to a graceful timber-roofed mosque. The local agency responsible for conservation could assist the mosque communities by offering design assistance and information on suitable products. There should be flexibility in understanding the unique economic situation of each mosque. The goal should be maintenance and conservation, in the spirit of renewal. Manoeuvring between historic preservation and the realities of the street is a delicate balancing act.

The timber mosques deserve consideration as unique byproducts of centuries of trade on the Indian Ocean. The monsoon ports and their hinterlands had very specific climatic conditions and an abundance of common and appropriate building materials. Monsoon mosques share a history, a method of timber construction methods, and a celebration of the roof. They bear witness to respectful coexistence. The regional variations are distinctive; the whole a marvel of inimitable grace. The old mosques we see today are evidence of the constant adjustment required to meet the needs of the faith, while remaining faithful to local building practices. As Asia embraces the 21st century, there is an urgent need for conservation to become a relevant, integral part of life. The revival of the monsoon mosque is a first step in embracing the wisdom of forbearers and the celebration of history.

Acknowledgements

As a girl growing up in the port city of New Orleans I was always fascinated by the docks: the looming hulls of the ships, the masses of cargo being moved from ship to dock, from dock to ship, the smell of all the stuff evoking elements of faraway places, the implied mysteries of voyages to distant lands. My father was employed by one of New Orleans major shipping companies and often he needed to visit a ship on Saturday. I would accompany him and be awed by everything: gangplanks and big men and scents of cotton, bananas, spices, coffee, muddy waters, engine fuel, workingmen, river breezes.

The youngest of the author's guides.

I could imagine sailing the seas, seeing the world, smelling the stuff of the Caribbean and points south.

So, of course, when I first started my investigations into the tropical timber mosques, I was especially intrigued by their connection to trade—the spice trade, the cloth trade, the movement of culture and people. Even though Islam, India and Indonesia were far from my beginnings I understood trade and movement and the mixing of cultures. As an architect I understand the importance of using what you have, of reflecting where you are, of creating spaces that inspire. And as an architect of the Pacific northwest I know about the beauty of wood, the possibilities of connections and the strength of wooden structures.

Although I had swooned over the tiled and domed mosques of the Middle East, I could not resist the simple beauty of the tropical mosques. What I could not understand was why they were so little recognized, so unknown and un-appreciated. From my first experience in open-air prayers in Penang, Malaysia, I knew that these were special places. Luckily, I was able to dive deep in my explorations of the tropical mosque. In 2007, with the cooperation of Dr Rajan Chedembath of Cochin's Centre for Heritage, Environment and Development, I received a Ford Foundation Grant to study the old mosques of Cochin. That work resulted in *Mosques of Cochin*. My inspiring friend Khoo Salma Nasution pushed me into considering a bigger book that included mosques from all along the tropical spice trade. This book includes portions of my first book as I have woven the Cochin mosques into the fabric of *Monsoon Mosques*.

I wish to thank all the people who assisted me as I travelled through Java and Sumatra, and returned to Kerala and Penang. The following are a few:
In Java: Gunawan Tjahjono, Punto Wijayanto, Bambang Setia Budi, Widya Wijayanti.
In Sumatra: Eko Alvares, Ariyati, Jonny Wongso.
In Kerala: Anoop Skaria and Dorrie Younger, Jiju, Surya Noufal, Feroze Babu, Kasthurba, Amritha Rajan, Anita Choudhuri, Vinod Cyriac, Rajan Chedembath, Luxmi, Fahed Majeed, Arshia Haq, Thoufeek Zakriya.
In Malaysia: Abdur-Razzaq Lubis and Khoo Salma Nasution.
In the US, the following provided advice, edits and encouragement: Manish Chalana, Shweta Bhatia Gupta, Desiana Pauli Sandjaja, Benjamin Fels and an incredibly generous donor.

I am very grateful to Gunawan Tjahjono, Punto Wijayanto and Abdur-Razzaq Lubis for their early readings and comments, and to the University of Washington Library, an outstanding institution and staff, which has hosted my research over the last decade.

Special thanks to Bipin Shah and his staff at Mapin Publishing.

There are so many more who I think about as I write, remembering their help, their observations and their welcome to their city, their mosque, their home.

More than anyone I thank Don Fels. He kept me company on all my travels, conscientiously took beautiful photographs, helped clarify my observations and inspired me to always smile.

Bibliography

Abdurrahman, K.V. *Brief Stories about the Mappila History*. Ponnani: Muslim Service Society, 1998.

Abdur Rahim, Khawaja (ed.) *Iqbal, the Poet of Tomorrow*. Lahore, 1968

Abu-Lughod, Janet. *Before European Hegemony*. New York: Oxford University Press, 1989.

———. "Creating one's future from one's past: nondefensively". *Traditional Dwellings and Settlements Review*. Vol. 7, No 1, 1995, p 7-11.

Adhi Moersid, Achmad Fanani, and Tulus Setyo Budhi. "Changes in the Islamic Religion and their Effects on the Built Environment." In *Understanding Islamic Architecture*. London: Routledge, 2002.

Adnan, Izrin Muaz Md. "A History of the Acheen Street Malay Enclave from Oral History Accounts." *Journal of the Malaysian Branch of the Royal Asiatic Society*, vol. 85, no. 1 (302), 2012

Akkach, Samar. *Cosmology and Architecture in Premodern Islam*. Albany: SUNY Press, 2005.

Ahmad Ibrahim, Sharon Siddique, Yasmin Hussain (eds.) *Readings on Islam in Southeast Asia*. Singapore: Institute of Southeast Asian Studies, 1985.

Alfieri, Bianca Maria. *Islamic Architecture of the Indian Subcontinent*. London: Laurence King, 2000.

Alexander, Christopher. *Notes on the Synthesis of Form*. Cambridge: Harvard University Press, 1964.

Ambary, Hasan Muarif. *Some Aspects of Islamic Architecture in Indonesia*. Pusat Penelitian Arkeologi Nasional, 1994.

Appleyard, Donald (ed.) *The Conservation of European Cities*. Cambridge, Mass: The MIT Press, 1979.

Aryanti, Desy. "Surau Syekh Burhanuddin Ulakan, Pariaman and Islamization of Minangkabau." *Diaspora Minang*, 2014.

Asher, Catherine and Cynthia Talbot. *India before Europe*. New York: Cambridge University Press, 2006.

Balagopal, T. S. Prabhu. "Kerala Architecture." In *Essays on the Cultural Formation of Kerala*. ed. P.J. Cherian. Thiruvananthapuram: Kerala Council for Historical Research, 1999.

Ballhatchet, Kenneth & David Taylor (eds.) *Changing South Asia: City and Culture*. Hong Kong: Asian Research Service, 1984.

Bastea, Eleni (ed.) *Memory and Architecture*. Albuquerque: University of New Mexico Press, 2004.

Bayly, Susan. *Saints, Goddesses and Kings*. Cambridge: Cambridge University Press, 1989.

Benda, Harry J. & Larkin, John A. (eds.) *The World of Southeast Asia*. New York: Harper & Row, 1967.

Bhatia, Gautam. *Laurie Baker: Life, Work, Writings*. New Delhi: Penguin Books, 1994.

Blair, Sheila & Jonathan Bloom (eds.) *Rivers of Paradise*. New Haven: Yale University Press, 2009.

Boyer, M. Christine. *The City of Collective Memory*. Cambridge, Mass: The MIT Press, 1994.

Brakel, L.F. & H. Massarik. "A Note on the Panjunan Mosque in Cirebon." *Archipel*, V 23, 1982, p 119-134.

Braudel, Fernand. *A History of Civilizations*. New York: Penguin Press, 1993.

Brierley, Joanna Hall. *Spices, The Story of Indonesia's Spice Trade*. Kuala Lumpur: Oxford University Press, 1994.

Bruce, Alan. "Notes on Early Mosques of the Malaysian Peninsula." *Journal of the Malayan Branch of the Royal Asiatic Society*, v69, No 2, 1996, p71-81.

Budi, Bambang Setia. "A Study on the History and Development of the Javanese Mosque Part 1." *Journal of Asian Architecture and Building Engineering*, v3, No1, May 2004.

———. "A Study on the History and Development of the Javanese Mosque Part 2." JAABE, v4, No1, May 2005.

———. "A Study on the History and Development of the Javanese Mosque Part 3." JAABE, 2006.

——— and Arif Sarwo Wibowo. "A typological Study of Historical Mosques in West Sumatra, Indonesia." JAABE, v17, No1, January 2018.

Cantacuzino, Sherban (ed.) *Architecture in Continuity, Building in the Islamic World Today*. New York: Aperture, 1985.

Capistrano, Florina Hernandez. *Reconstructing the past: The notion of tradition in west Sumatran architecture, 1791-1991*. PhD Thesis, Columbia University, 1997.

Chaudhuri, K.N. *Trade and Civilisation in the Indian Ocean*. Cambridge: Cambridge University Press, 1985.

———. *Asia Before Europe*. Cambridge: Cambridge University Press, 1990.

Coedes, G. *The Indianized States of Southeast Asia*. Ed. Walter F. Vella, trans. Susan Brown Cowing. Honolulu: University of Hawai'i, 1968.

Collet, Octave J.A. *Terres et Peuples de Sumatra*. Amsterdam, 1925.

Correa, Charles. *A Place in the Shade: The New Landscape and Other Essays*. Hatje Cantz, 2012.

Cortesao, Armando (ed. and trans.) *The Suma Oriental of Tome Pires*. 2 vols. London: Hakluyt Society, 1944.

Cribb, Robert. *Historical Atlas of Indonesia*. Richmond: Curzon Press, 2000.

Dale, Stephen Frederic. *Islamic Society on the South Asian Frontier. The Mappilas of Malabar*. Oxford: Clarendon Press, 1980.

———. "Trade, Conversion and the Growth of the Islamic Community of Kerala, South India." *Studia Islamica*, No. 71 (1990), pp 155.175.

Das Gupta, Ashin. *Malabar in Asian Trade 1740-1800*. Cambridge: Cambridge University Press, 1967.

Dawson, Barry and John Gillow. *The Traditional Architecture of Indonesia*. London: Thames and Hudson, 1994.

Day, Francis. *The Land of the Permauls or Cochin Its Past and Its Present*, 1863. Reprint, New Delhi: Asian Educational Services, 1990.

De Graaf, H.J. "The Origin of the Javanese Mosque." *Journal of Southeast Asian History*, Vol 4, No 1 (March 1963).

Desai, Miki. "Wooden Architecture of Kerala: The Physicality and the Spirituality." *Traditional and Vernacular Architecture*. Chennai: Madras Craft Foundation, 2003.

Dobbin, Christine. *Islamic Revivalism in a Changing Peasant Economy*. London: Curzon Press, 1983.

Dobby, E.H.G. *Monsoon Asia*. Chicago: Quadrangle Books, 1961

Dumarcay, Jacques. *Architecture and its Models in South-East Asia*. Bangkok: Orchid Press, 2003.

———. *Construction Techniques in South and Southeast Asia*. Leiden: Brill, 2005.

———. "La charpenterie des mosquées javanaises." *Archipel*, vol 30 (1985) pp. 21-30.

———. *Histoire de l'architecture de Java*. Paris: Ecole Francaise d'Extreme Orient, 1993.

Dunn, Ross E. *The Adventures of Ibn Battuta. A Muslim Traveler of the 14th Century*. Revised edition, Berkeley: University of California Press, 2005.

Eaton, Richard M. (ed.) *India's Islamic Traditions, 711-1750*. New Delhi: Oxford University Press, 2003.

Engineer, Asghar Ali (ed.) *Kerala Muslims A Historical Perspective*. New Delhi: Ajanta Publications, 1995.

Fathurahman, Oman. "Reinforcing Neo-Sufism in the Malay-Indonesian World: Shaṭṭārīyah Order in West Sumatra." *Studia Islamika,* Vol.10 (3), 2003, pp. 29-93.

Feener, R. Michael & Terenjit Sevea (eds.) *Islamic Connections*. Singapore: ISEAS Publishing, 2009.

Fels, Patricia Tusa. *Mosques of Cochin*. Ahmedabad: Mapin Publishing, 2011.

Fergusson, James. *History of Indian and Eastern Architecture*. London: J. Murray, 1910

Fort Cochin Mattancherry, A Study of Space and Society. Dept of Architecture, Trivandrum, 1995-6.

Florida, Nancy. *Writing the Past, Inscribing the Future*. Durham: Duke University Press, 1995.

Frishman, Martin & Hasan-Uddin Khan (eds.) *The Mosque*. London: Thames and Hudson, 1994.

Galeano, Eduardo. *Memory of Fire: I. Genesis*. Trans. Cedric Belfrage. New York: Pantheon Books, 1985.

———. *Mirrors*. New York: Nation Books, 2009.

Gayle, Leslee. *Applied decorative design on handwoven cloth inspired by the textiles of Sumatra, Indonesia*. Masters Thesis, University of Alberta, 1989.

Geertz, Clifford. *Islam Observed*. New Haven: Yale University Press, 1968.

———. *The Religion of Java*. London: Collier-Macmillan, 1960.

———. *After the Fact*. Cambridge: Harvard University Press, 1995.

———. *Available Light*. Princeton: Princeton University Press, 2000

Ghosh, Amitav. *In an Antique Land*. New Delhi: Ravi Dayal Publisher, 1992.

———. *The Iman and the Indian*. New Delhi: Ravi Dayal Publisher, 2002.

Gilmartin, David and Bruce B. Lawrence (eds.) *Beyond Turk and Hindu. Rethinking Religious Identities in Islamicate South Asia*. Gainesville: University Press of Florida, 2000.

Griswold, Eliza. *The Tenth Parallel*. New York: Farrar, Straus & Giroux, 2010.

Gupta, Anirudha (ed.) *Minorities on India's West Coast*. New Delhi: Kalinga Publications, 1991.

Hadler, Jeffrey. *Muslims and Matriarchs*. Ithaca: Cornell University Press, 2008.

Haidar, Mansura (ed.) *Sufis, Sultans and Feudal Orders*. New Delhi: Manohar, 2004.

Hamdouni Alami, Mohammed. *Art and Architecture in the Islamic Tradition*. London: I.B. Tauris, 2011.

Haryadi. "Conservation of cultural settings: the case of Yogyakarta's inner city kampung." *Cultural Identity and Urban Change in Southeast Asia*. Deakin University Press, 1994.

Heringa, Rens, et al. *Fabric of Enchantment. Batik from the North Coast of Java*. Los Angeles: Los Angeles County Museum of Art, 1996.

Ho, Engseng. *The Graves of Tarim*. Berkeley: University of California Press, 2006.

Horovitz, J. *List of the Published Mohamedan Inscriptions of India. Epigraphia Indo-Moslemica 1909-10*. New Delhi, Archaeological Survey of India, 1987.

Hoskins, Janet. *Biographical Objects*. New York: Routledge, 1998.

Hourani, George Fadlo. *Arab Seafaring in the Indian Ocean in Ancient and Early Medieval Times*. Princeton: Princeton University Press, 1951.

Iqbal, Muhammad. *Poems from Iqbal*. Trans. V.G. Kiernan. London: John Murray, 1955.

Jogja Heritage Society. *Homeowner's Conservation Manual*. Jakarta: UNESCO, 2007.

Kaplan, Robert D. *Monsoon*. New York: Random House, 2010.

Karim, Wazir Jahan, ed. *Straits Muslims: Diasporas of the Northern Passage of the Straits of Malacca*. INAS, Straits G.T., Penang, 2009.

Katakam, Ramu. *Glimpses of Architecture in Kerala*. New Delhi: Rupa & Co, 2006.

Katkova, Irina. "Searching for Islamic Manuscripts in Western Sumatra", *IIAS Newsletter*, # 46 Winter 2008.

Kasthurba, A.K. *Kuttichira – A Medieval Muslim Settlement of Kerala*. Calicut: Malabar Institute for Research & Development, 2012.

Kern, R.A. "The Origin of the Malay Surau." *Journal of the Malayan Branch of the Royal Asiatic Society*, Vol 29, N 1 (173) May 1956, 179-181.

Khan, Ahmad Nabi. *Islamic Architecture in South Asia*. Oxford: Oxford University Press, 2003.

Khoo Salma Nasution. *The Chulia in Penang: Patronage and Place-Making around the Kapitan Kling Mosque*. Penang Malaysia: Areca Books, 2014.

King, Anthony D. *Spaces of Global Cultures*. London: Routledge, 2004.

Kleinsteuber, A., & Maharadjo, Syafri M. *Masjid-masjid kuno di Indonesia : Warisan budaya dari masa ke masa = Old mosques in Indonesia : Cultural heritage through the times*. Jakarta: Genta Kreasi Nusantara, 2012.

Knapp, Ronald G. (ed.) *Asia's Old Dwellings*. Hong Kong: Oxford University Press, 2003.

Kuncoro, Indah Sulistiana. "Documentation on Reroofing Tradition in Kabuyutan Trusmi, Cirebon" ACCU Nara The Eleventh Regular Report, UNESCO.

Kusno, Abidin. *Behind the Postcolonial*. New York: Routledge, 2000.

———. *The Appearance of Memory*. Durham: Duke University Press, 2010.

———, ed. "Gunawan Tjahjono & Josef Prijotomo, Postcolonial Traditionality." *Inaugural Speeches in the Built Environment*. Delft, 2017.

———. "Invisible Geographies in the Study of Islamic Architecture." *International Journal of Islamic Architecture*, 5(2016), 29-35.

Laffan, Michael. *The Makings of Indonesian Islam*. Princeton: Princeton University Press, 2011.

Lape, Peter. "Archaeological approaches to the study of Islam in Island Southeast Asia." Antiquity, 79 (2005) 829-36.

Lee Chor Lin. *Batik, Creating an Identity*. National Museum of Singapore and Editions Didier Millet, 1997 & 2007.

Leigh, Barbara. "Design Motifs in Aceh: Indian and Islamic Influences." *The Malay Islamic World of Sumatra*. Monash University, 1982.

Loeb, Edwin M. *Sumatra, Its History and People*. Kuala Lumpur: Oxford University Press, 1972. (1st pub. 1935)

Logan, William, *Malabar Manual*, 2 vols. Reprint, New Delhi: Asian Educational Services, 2000.

Lubis, Abdur Razzaq & Khoo Salma Nasution. *Raja Bilah and the Mandailings in Perak: 1875-1911*. MBRAS, 2003.

Lubis, Abdur Razzaq. *Sutan Puasa Founder of Kuala Lumpur*. Penang Malaysia: Areca Books, 2018.

Mackintosh-Smith, T. *The hall of a thousand columns: Hindustan to Malabar with Ibn Battutah*. London: John Murray, 2005.

Malekandathil, Pius. *Portuguese Cochin and the Maritime Trade of India 1500-1663*. New Delhi: Manohar, 2001.

Malieckal, Bindu. "Muslims, Matriliny, and A Midsummer Night's Dream: European Encounters with the Mapplilas of Malabar, India." *The Muslim World*, Vol 95, April 2005, p 297-316

Mathew, K.S. (ed.) *Maritime Malabar and The Europeans, 1500-1962*. Haryana: Hope India Publications, 2003.

Mayaram, Shail, M.S.S. Pandian & Ajay Skaria, editors. *Muslims Dalits and the Fabrications of History*. London: Seagull Books, 2006.

Metcalf, Barbara D. (ed.) *Islam in South Asia in Practice*. Princeton: Princeton University Press, 2009.

Metcalf, Barbara D. & Thomas R Metcalf. *A Concise History of India*. Cambridge: Cambridge University Press, 2002.

Metcalf, Thomas R. *An Imperial Vision*. Berkeley: University of California Press, 1989.

Miksic, John. *Singapore and the Silk Road of the Sea*. Singapore: NUS Press, 2013.

———. "Urbanization and Social Change: The Case of Sumatra." *Archipel*, Vol 37, 1989, pp 3-29.

Miller, Roland E. *Mappila Muslims of Kerala*. New Delhi: Orient Longman, 1976.

Mohamad, Goenawan. *Conversations with Difference*. Jakarta: PT Tempo, 2002.

———. *Selected Poems*. Selangor: Katakita, 2004.

Naipaul, V.S. *Beyond Belief*. London: Little, Brown & Co., 1998.

Nalbantoglu, G.B. and C.T. Wong (eds.) *Postcolonial spaces*. New York: Princeton Architectural Press, 1997.

Nas, Peter J.M. (ed.) *The Past in the Present, Architecture in Indonesia*. Leiden: KITLV Press, 2007.

Nasr, Seyyed Hossein. *Islam in the Modern World*. New York: Harper Collins, 2010.

Nizami, Khaliq Ahmad. *Religion and Politics in India during the 13th Century*, 1961. Reprint, New Delhi: Oxford University Press, 2002.

Oliver, Paul (ed.) *Shelter, Sign & Symbol*. Woodstock, NY: The Overlook Press, 1977.

Oliver, Paul. *Shelter & Society, Primitive Dwelling and Vernacular Architecture*. New York: Frederick A Praeger, 1969.

O'Neill, Hugh. "Islamic Architecture under the New Order." *Culture and Society in New Order Indonesia*, ed. Virginia Matheson Hooker. Kuala Lumpur: Oxford University Press, 1993.

Peacock, A.C.S. & Annabel Teh Gallop (eds.) *From Anatolia to Aceh*. Oxford: Oxford University Press, 2015.

Pearson, M.N. ed. *Spices in the Indian Ocean World*. Brookfield, VT: Variorum, 1996.

Pemberton, John. *On the Subject of Java*. Ithaca: Cornell University Press, 1994.

Pigeaud, Theodore G. Th. *Islamic States in Java 1500-1700, Vol IV*. The Hague: Martinus Nijhoff, 1976.

Pisani, Elizabeth. *Indonesia Etc*. London: Granta Publications, 2014.

Pramar, V.S. *A Social History of Indian Architecture*. New Delhi: Oxford University Press, 2005

Prasad, N. Devi. *Fort Cochin & Mattancherry A Monograph*. New Delhi: INTACH, 1994.

Prijotomo, Josef. *Ideas and Forms of Javanese Architecture*. Yogyakarta: Gadjah Mada University Press, 1984.

Randathani, Husain (ed.) *Makdhoomum Ponnaniyum*. Ponnani: Ponnani Juma Masjid Committee, 1998

Rasdi, Mohamad Tajuddin Mohamad. "Mosque Architecture in Malaysia: Classification of Styles and Possible Influence" *Journal Alam Bina*

Reid, Anthony. *Southeast Asia in the Age of Commerce 1450-1680*. New Haven: Yale University Press, 1988.

———, (ed.) *Southeast Asia in the Early Modern Era*. Ithaca: Cornell University Press, 1993.

———. *Indonesia Rising: The Repositioning of Asia's Third Giant*. Singapore: Institute of SE Asian Studies, 2012.

———. "Southeast Asian Consumption of Indian and British Cotton Cloth", in Riello, Giorgio and Tirthankar Roy (eds.), *How India Clothed the World* (Leiden: Brill, 2009) pp. 31-51.

Risso, Patricia. *Merchants and Faith*. Boulder: Westview Press, 1995.

Rodgers, Susan (ed.) *Telling Lives, Telling History*. Berkeley: University of California Press, 1995.

Rujivacharakul, V., Hahn, H. Hazel, Oshima, Ken Tadashi, & Christensen, Peter. (eds) *Architecturalized Asia: Mapping a continent through history*. Honolulu: University of Hawai'i Press, 2013.

Rushdie, Salman. *The Moor's Last Sigh*. London: Vintage, 1997. (1st pub 1995)

Said, Edward W. *Orientalism*. New York: Vintage Books, 1979.

Salleh Mohd. Akib. *Masjid Tua Kampung Laut*. Kota Bharu, 2003.

Samad, Dr. M. Abdul. *Islam in Kerala*. Kollam: Laurel Publications, 1998.

Sanyal, Sanjeev. *Land of the Seven Rivers*. Guragon, India: Penguin Books, 2012.

Sarai Reader 02: The Cities of Everyday Life. New Delhi: Center for the Study of Developing Societies, 2002.

Sarkar, H. *Monuments of Kerala*. New Delhi: Archaeological Survey of India, 1992.

Schildt, Henri. *Traditional Kerala Manor*. Institut Francais de Pondicherry, 2012.

Md. Sharif, Harlina. *Mosques in island Southeast Asia, 15th–20th century*. PhD Thesis. SOAS, University of London, 2013.

Shokoohy, Mehrdad. *Muslim Architecture of South India*. London: RoutledgeCurzon, 2003.

Suárez, T. *Early Mapping of Southeast Asia*. Singapore: Periplus Editions, 1999.

Subrahmanyam, Sanjay. *Explorations In Connected History: From the Tagus to the Ganges*. New Delhi: Oxford University Press, 2005.

Sugiharta, Sri. *Masjid Kuna*. 2005.

Summerfield, Anne & John (eds). *Walk In Splendor*. Los Angeles: UCLA Fowler Museum of Cultural History, 1999.

Sutherland, Heather. "Geography as destiny? The role of water in Southeast Asian history." In Peter Boomgaard, ed. *A World of Water*, pp. 27-70. Leiden: KITLV Press, 2007.

Tajudeen, Imran bin. "Java's Architectural Enigma: The Austronesian World and the Limits of Asia". In *Architecturalized Asia: Mapping a continent through history*. Editors Rujivacharakul, V… Honolulu: University of Hawai'i Press, 2013.

Thampuran, Ashalatha. *Traditional Architectural Forms of Malabar Coast*. Kozhikode: Vastuvidyapratisthanam, 2001.

Tibbetts, G.R. *A Study of the Arabic Texts Containing material on South-East Asia*. Leiden: E.J. Brill, 1979.

Tillotson, G.H.R. (ed.) *Paradigms of Indian Architecture*. Richmond, Surrey: Curzon Press, 1998

———. *The Tradition of Indian Architecture*. New Haven and London: Yale University Press, 1989

Tjahjono, Gunawan (ed.) *Indonesian Heritage: Architecture*. Singapore: Archipelago Press, 1998

———. *Cosmos, Center, and Duality in Javanese Architectural Tradition: The Symbolic Dimensions of House Shapes in Koto Gede and Surroundings*. Thesis, Ph.D. Architecture, University of California, Berkeley, 1989

Tjandrasasmita, Uka. *Growth and Development of Moslem Coastal Cities in Indonesia from the 13th-18th Century*. Center for Research and Development, 2012.

———. *Islamic Antiquities of Sendang Duwur*. Jakarta: The Archaeological Foundation, 1975.

Tjoa-Bonatz, Mai Lin et al. "Early Architectural Images from Muara Jambi, on Sumatra, Indonesia." *Asian Perspectives*, vol 48, No 1 (Spring 2009): 32-55.

Toer, P. *Footsteps*. Harmondsworth: Penguin,1990.

Van Beek, Aart. *Life in the Javanese Kraton*. Singapore: Oxford University Press, 1990.

Vellinga, Marcel. *Constituting unity and difference. Vernacular architecture in a Minangkabau village*. Leiden: KITLV Press, 2004.

Visser, Margaret. *The Geometry of Love*. HarperCollins, 2000.

Wahby, Ahmed E.I. The Architecture of the Early Mosques and Shrines of Java: Influences of the Arab Merchants in the 15th and 16th Centuries? Dissertation, 2007.

Wallace, Alfred Russel. *The Malay Archipelago*. Singapore: Oxford University Press, 1991 (1st ed.1869).

Waterson, Roxana. *The Living House: An Anthology of Architecture in South-East Asia*. Singapore: Oxford University Press, 1990.

Wheatley, Paul. *The Golden Khersonese: Studies in the Historical Geography of the Malay Peninsula before AD 1500*. Kuala Lumpur: University of Malaya Press, 1961.

Wink, Andre. "From the Mediterranean to the Indian Ocean: Medieval History in Geographical Perspective." *Comparative Studies in Society and History*, Vol 44, No 3 (Jul 2002): 416-445.

Wiryomartono, Bagoes. "A Historical View of Mosque Architecture in Indonesia." *Asia Pacific Journal of Anthropology*, Vol 10, No 1 (2009): 33-45.

Wolpert, Stanley. *A New History of India*, 5th ed. New York: Oxford University Press, 1997.

Wolters, O.W. *History, Culture, and Region in Southeast Asian Perspectives*. Singapore: Institute of SE Asian Studies, 1982.

Woodward, Mark W. *Islam in Java: Normative Piety and Mysticism in the Sultanate of Yogyakarta*. Tucson: University of Arizona Press, 1989.

Wurster, William and Catherine Bauer. "Indian Vernacular Architecture: Wai and Cochin." *Perspecta*, Vol 5 (1959) p 36-48.

Shaykh Zainuddin Makhdum. *Tuhfat al-Mujahidin*. Trans. S. Muhammad Husayn Nainar. Calicut: Other Books, 2006.